around NEW YORK CITY *with* KIDS

by Paul Eisenberg

Credits
Writer: Paul Eisenberg

Editors: Susan MacCallum-Whitcomb, Maria Teresa Hart
Editorial Production: Evangelos Vasilakis
Production Manager: Angela L. Mclean

Design: Fabrizio La Rocca, *creative director*
Cover Art and Design: Jessie Hartland
Flip Art and Illustration: Rico Lins, Keren Ora Adomoni/ Rico Lins Studio

About the Writer
A native New Yorker, Paul Eisenberg is a Lowell Thomas Award–winning journalist who serves as family vacation blogger for Shermans Travel and as editor of the website Traveling Dad. He was formerly editorial director at Fodor's. His writing has appeared in *Nick Jr.* magazine, the *New York Daily News*, the *New York Press*, and New York.com. He lives in New York City with his wife and three children.

Fodor's Around New York City with Kids

Sixth Edition
ISBN 978-0-89141-972-3
ISSN 1526-1468

An Important Tip and an Invitation
Although all prices, opening times, and other details in this book are based on information supplied to us as of this writing, changes occur all the time in the travel world, and Fodor's cannot accept responsibility for facts that become outdated or for inadvertent errors or omissions. So always confirm information when it matters, especially if you're making a detour to visit a specific place. Your experiences— positive and negative—matter to us. If we have missed or misstated something, please write to us. We follow up on all suggestions. Contact the Around New York City with Kids editor at editors@fodors.com or c/o Fodor's at 1745 Broadway, New York, New York 10019.

Special Sales
This book is available for special discounts for bulk purchases for sales promotions or premiums. Special editions, including personalized covers, excerpts of existing books, and corporate imprints, can be created in large quantities for special needs. For more information, write to Special Markets/Premium Sales, 1745 Broadway, MD 3-1, New York, New York 10019, or e-mail specialmarkets@randomhouse. com.

PRINTED IN THE UNITED STATES OF AMERICA
10 9 8 7 6 5 4 3 2 1

FUN TIMES A TO Z

GET READY, GET SET!

And just let go.

Let go of the idea that you have to see all 68 things in this book. It is, in every sense, just a guide.

Let go of the expectation that you are going to see every part of every thing in this book. Take Central Park, for instance. There are native New Yorkers who were practically raised there and who are practically raising their own kids there. And you know what? Those kids-turned-parents still haven't seen the whole park and their kids likely won't either. It's just the way it is.

Let go, because if you insist on checking off the sites in this guidebook like it's a checklist, or if you pressure your family to spend five minutes apiece seeing four galleries at the Natural History museum when you know in your heart they would have been far happier spending just 20 minutes in one of them, then you may be missing the point of being here.

In other words, don't miss everything while you're seeing it all.

Let go. Let your kids be kids and enjoy their time here. And you enjoy, too! Please. Have that cold draft or warm cookie. See just a few of the sites (and of those, Facebook your favorites, not all of them). And know you'll be back. At least we hope so.

A few more things to keep in mind as you and your kids make your way through this book and through New York City:

LOOK INSIDE (EVEN BEFORE YOU BUY. IT'S OKAY, GO AHEAD.)

Each two-page spread in this book describes a great place to take your family. The "toolbar" at the top of the page lists all the particulars: address, phone numbers, websites, admission prices, hours, age recommendations, and subway stops. (Yes, the subway! You can do it!) **"Make the Most of Your Time"** boxes offer practical information that will help you save time, minimize aggravation, and perhaps even save you a little money; **"Eats for Kids"** identifies family-friendly restaurants and eateries near the sights; and **"Keep in Mind"** gives additional travel tips about the site or neighborhood.

To get started, just flip through the book, keeping an eye peeled for the Statue of Liberty's magical transformation. Now let your kid flip through it.

When you finally get the book back, you'll find places of interest to your family by just leafing through the listings (in alphabetical order) or by looking in the directories in the front and back of the book. "All Around Town" groups sights by neighborhood, helpful if you're planning to visit more than one attraction or are looking for additional kid-friendly dining choices. "Something for Everyone" groups attractions by type, such as parks and gardens or free attractions. And speaking of free . . .

SAVE A LITTLE DOUGH
The easiest way to save money here is through free admission to popular museums and other not-for-profit institutions. Often museums have one night per week or per month when you can get in at no charge.

Are you a member of museum at home that has a reciprocal relationship with one of ours? Check that one out.

Do you work for a company that is a sponsor of an institution? If you don't know, call someone in HR. They love it when you use company benefits. At many points of interest, including several listed in this book, you may be able to get in for free by showing your company ID. On the subject of ID cards, don't forget that if you are or were in the armed forces, are a senior, a student, or a member of AAA, you could be entitled to a discount.

We've tried to list above-average sandwich and snack-type joints along with sit-down meal places. And several of the sit-down restaurants listed in this book, as well as others you encounter, may have prix-fixe lunch specials.

Don't feel you have to eat somewhere, or eat at all, just because we've put the idea in your head. Nor do you have to eat lunch at lunchtime. Blow off the midday meal and have snacks at 3:30 PM; then eat again at 10 PM. You're on vacation, remember? Do try to start the day with a real breakfast, though, instead of a half-eaten cereal bar. You're not at home, remember?

We've tried to put our favorite free experiences in this book. Our favorite newest one since the last edition? The High Line. Governor's Island. Carl Schurz Park. Walking tours of Union Square Park and Chinatown's Mott Street, Okay, we admit it. As with our children, we love them all equally.

But really, the High Line is awesome.

DON'T FORGET TO WRITE

Is there an attraction in our countdown that your family especially enjoys? Did we overlook one of your favorite places? We'd love to hear from you. Send your emails to me c/o editors@fodors.com. Please include "Around New York City with Kids" in the subject line. Or drop me a line by snail mail c/o Around New York City with Kids, Fodor's Travel Publications, 1745 Broadway, New York, NY 10019.

Happy traveling!

—Paul Eisenberg

BEST BETS

BEST IN TOWN
American Museum of Natural History **68**
Bronx Zoo **65**
Central Park **57**
Coney Island **52**
High Line **43**

BEST OUTDOORS
Brooklyn Bridge and DUMBO **63**
Central Park **57**
Coney Island **52**
Governor's Island **47**
High Line **43**

BEST CULTURAL ACTIVITY
Broadway on a Budget **66**
Carnegie Hall **59**
Guggenheim **44**
New Victory Theater **29**
Symphony Space **6**

BEST MUSEUM
American Museum of Natural History **68**
Guggenheim **44**
Metropolitan Museum of Art **36**
Museum of the Moving Image **32**
New-York Historical Society **23**

WACKIEST
Coney Island **52**
Madame Tussauds Wax Museum **37**
Ripley's Believe It Or Not **14**
Sony Wonder Technology Lab **10**

SOMETHING FOR EVERYONE

ALL AROUND TOWN

Even locals who come here regularly haven't managed to explore every nook and cranny of this museum. So you shouldn't expect to tackle it all on a single trip. Take your time and savor what you can, because inevitably you'll be back.

That said, if it is your family's first visit and it's going to be your only visit for a while, you'll want to hit some highlights. Start with Fossil Hall, the world's largest collection of vertebrate fossils. Of the museum's 1 million fossils, 85% are the real thing—not casts—which is often the first question asked about this collection. Watch the evolution film if attention spans permit, otherwise follow the dino tracks to the two halls of the dinosaur wing where you'll spy favorites like the towering T-Rex, the Velociraptor head, and the Allosaurus making quick work of a carcass.

Also essential are the classic glass dioramas in the Akeley Hall of African Mammals. The Alaskan Brown Bear and African elephants can be studied down to their whiskers.

KEEP IN MIND If you can pull your kids away from the tempting gift shop, visit **Maxilla & Mandible** (451 Columbus Ave., tel. 212/724–6173). An emporium of natural items unlike any other, this shop holds piles of shells, fossils, bones, and bugs—almost all of which are real (well, except the human bones). Kids may find something they'll treasure for as little as $1, but most people find it's fun just to window shop here.

Central Park West at 79th St.
Subway: 1 to 79th St.;
B (weekdays only), C to 81st St.

 212/769-5100, 212/769-5200
reservations; www.amnh.org

 Suggested donation $19 ages 13 and
up, $10.50 children 2–12; museum and
planetarium space show $25 ages 13
and up, $14.50 children; IMAX extra

Daily 10–5:45, space
shows daily 10:30–4

 2 and up

Don't miss the lower level of the Rose Center, where six-year-olds and teens alike delight in leaping on the floor scales to check their weight on other planets. If it's your first time, definitely catch a show in the Hayden Planetarium (though be mindful that the theater's dark "night sky" might be a little intimidating for little ones). Right next door, the Hall of Gems wows girls and boys equally not just with its diamonds, opals, and the world's larges sapphire, but with the capacity of the carpet here to deliver electric shocks. The Whale Room (aka Hall of Biodiversity) astounds even the most jaded visitor with its life-size blue whale hovering over other ocean life dioramas.

Finally, a favorite for the under-eight set is the Discovery Room, where they can open doors and drawers to touch shells, insects, and more. Upstairs, older children can peer through microscopes for a close-up look at nature.

If you like this sight, you may also like the National Museum of the American Indian (#31).

MAKE THE MOST OF YOUR TIME

There's no shame in taking short breaks, especially if they'll prolong your stamina. The carpeted platforms in the serene Hall of Minerals are popular for sitting and, you might find, jumping, though the latter should be discouraged.

EATS FOR KIDS

The **Museum Food Court** serves a wider variety and better quality of food than your typical museum cafeteria, including the kid-standard mac-and-cheese, chicken fingers, and pizza. **Café on One** also offers quick gourmet sandwiches, tasty salads, and drinks. A rarity—a brunch place with ample room that gracefully serves lots of families—**Jacob's Pickles** (509 Amsterdam Ave., near 84th St., 212/470–5566) has kid- and grown-up-friendly biscuit sandwiches topped with yummy artery pleasers like fried chicken with sausage gravy and, for good measure, pickles.

BASKETBALL FOR KIDS

I f you're visiting between late October and April with a child who just happens to be obsessed with men's basketball, you've found one of your great things to do in this city.

New York is, of course, home to the Knicks at Madison Square Garden and the Brooklyn Nets (go black and white, yo!) at the Barclays Center, which opened in September 2012.

But first things first, let's manage expectations. If you're hoping to watch hoop action at the Garden, even the relatively cheap seats (home games from $55) are sold out well in advance, so your only realistic option for Knicks tickets (and most other NBA tickets) is to order them ahead of time. If that's not practical, it is possible to buy same-day seats at the Garden box office, though remaining tickets may be prohibitively expensive. If that's the case you might have better luck finding same-day tickets to a college basketball game: Highlights at the Garden include the Jimmy V Classic (tickets from $15) or April's National Invitation Tournament (NIT) with tix from $10.

MAKE THE MOST OF YOUR TIME

The debut of the Barclays Center has ignited excitement among Brooklyn business owners hoping to cash in on fans entering or emptying out of the arena. So during your visit you may well be a pioneer as you discover newly opening stores and restaurants.

EATS FOR KIDS Chain eateries abound around the Garden. But if you want a slightly better meal nearby, head to **Lugo Caffé** (1 Penn Plaza, tel. 212/760–2700) pregame, for eggplant caponata, Tuscan bean salad, or house-made pastas. At Barclays, Brooklyn Burger, Calexico, and Fatty Cue BBQ are among the 37 food vendors. If you want to wander just a block away from Barclays for a farm-to-table sit-down, try **Melt** (440 Bergen St., tel. 718/230–5925). It serves terrific brunch fare plus burgers, Swedish meatballs, and lobster mac-and-cheese for dinner.

Madison Square Garden 7th Ave. between 31 and 33rd Sts.; Barclays Center
620 Atlantic Ave., Brooklyn
Subway: Garden 1, 2, 3, A, C, E to 34th St./Penn Station; Barclays Center
2, 3, 4, 5, B, D N, Q, R to Atlantic Ave./Barclays Center

Prices vary
by team

Game times vary
by arena

6 and up

866/858–0008 Garden tickets, 917/618–6700 Barclays box
office; www.thegarden.com, www.barclayscenter.com

Your best bet, however, if you want to combine a spontaneous same-day ticket buy and check out a new point of interest in the city, is to head out to the Barclays Center in Brooklyn, the extremely proud home of the newly rebranded Brooklyn Nets (tickets from $22).

The reason snagging same-day seats at Barclays Center might work out is that less die-hard sports fans may as yet be unwilling to make the (easy) train trip to the Barclays Center, which is approximately 5 miles and a half hour from midtown Manhattan. Should you arrive at the box office and find tickets sold out, you could do a lot worse than kill a little time in and around the Barclays Center and its surrounding neighborhood.

If you like this sight, you may also like a ballgame at Yankee Stadium (#1).

KEEP IN MIND Renovations at the Garden have meant that the WNBA's New York Liberty home games (from $10) have been relocated to the Prudential Center in Newark, at least through the 2013 season. Should you be in town during the Liberty's season (Memorial Day weekend through August), it might be worth a side trip here, especially if you miss out on tickets at the New York arenas.

BROADWAY ON A BUDGET

Nobody living in New York City pays full price for Broadway tickets if they can help it. Neither should you, given how plentiful and accessible discounted tickets are.

You may already be familiar with TKTS ticket booths as a way to get 20%–50% off face-value tickets. Don't expect to see the newest hit show offered, but virtually anything running for a year or more will be available at some point. The most popular outlet (read: the one with the longest lines) is the Times Square Booth, which sits below a beautiful set of glass bleachers, giving a pep-rally view of Times Square. It sells day-of-performance tickets only. The South Street Seaport and Downtown Brooklyn booths sell tickets to evening performances on the day of, and matinees the day before. The latter also sells tickets to Brooklyn performing arts events. Follow their Twitter feed (twitter.com/tkts) for show availability before trudging out to these locations. There is a non-musicals line that is much shorter if you're seeing a play.

What you may not know is that the Theater Development Fund (the organization behind TKTS) runs a membership-based discount ticket service ($30 annually) providing advance

MAKE THE MOST OF YOUR TIME If you've ever hunted for online shopping coupons and discount codes, you'll be happy to know they exist for Broadway, too. Do an Internet search for "Discount Broadway Tickets" with the show's name, or search websites like www.broadwaybox.com before using any other method to get tickets. Broadway shows rarely go for under $55; so if you can snag anything less than that online, you will save yourself some dough as well as precious time standing in line or at the box office.

TKTS Times Square, Broadway and 47th St.; South Street Seaport, 199 Water St.; Downtown Brooklyn, 1 MetroTech Center, corner Jay St. and Myrtle Ave. Subway: 1, 2, 3, 7, N, Q, R, S to Times Square; Seaport 2, 3, 4, 5, J, Z to Fulton Street; A, C to Broadway–Nassau; Brooklyn A, C, F, R to Jay Street–MetroTech; 2, 3, 4, 5 to Court Street–Borough Hall

Usually 50%–75% off regular price plus $4 surcharge per ticket

212/912–9770; www.tdf.org

Duffy Sq. W–M 3–8, T 2–8, plus W and Sa 10–2, Su 11–3; Seaport M–Sa 11–6, Su 11–4, Brooklyn M–Sa 11–6; closed 3–3:30.

8 and up, varies by show

tickets to many Broadway shows for $11–$39 per ($9 for Off-Off-Broadway). Because it's open to students, teachers, union members, military, performing arts professionals, and more, chances are someone in your family qualifies.

The next best option is specialty or chance tickets. Many theaters offer Student Rush, Standing Room Only, and Lottery tickets. Check with individual theaters for policies and details. Seats can range from prime orchestra to partial-view. Students with ID can often get relatively cheap tickets—even to hit shows not otherwise discounted—by going to the box office at a specified time; check individual theaters for details. Lottery tickets are available to winners picked in a draw (each winner is entitled to 2). Anyone can get the limited availability SRO seats, which are usually designated standing areas behind the orchestra seats: They're typically available when the box office opens.

If you like Broadway, you may also like Symphony Space (#6).

EATS FOR KIDS Ninth Avenue has several good choices for families. A local favorite of sausage aficionados, **Hallo Berlin** (744 9th Ave., tel. 212/333–2372) is a good pick for finicky palates. For another quick bite, walk over to the World Financial Center (49th/50th St. at 8th/9th Aves.) with its outdoor tables and benches and get Kobe hamburgers and crisp fries at **Mother Burger** (329 W. 49th St., tel. 212/757–8600).

KEEP IN MIND Another way to save on long-running shows is to get a bookmark-shaped coupon that discounts select tickets by 20%–30%. They're distributed near store cash registers, near TKTS lines, and sometimes in city schools. Look for them at a local NYPL branch if all else fails.

BRONX ZOO

Even if you live near a mega-zoo, you all deserve a visit here. The East Coast's answer to the San Diego Zoo, this is the largest urban wildlife park in the U.S. (4,000+ animals) and one that takes a humane, cage-free approach.

Come early, allow plenty of time, and bring comfortable walking shoes; you could easily spend a full three days here and still not do it all.

Visit the most popular attractions in the morning when the crowds are thinnest. These include the African Plains with its giraffes, zebras, and lions; the Asian Jungle packed with tree kangaroos, otters, gibbons, and other impish creatures; and the always popular World of Reptiles with its often elusive nocturnal animals.

Particularly charming is the Mouse House. In a city where mice can often be spotted in unexpected places, it's unusual to find so many varieties welcome in one place. Mole rats, kangaroo rats (yes, they hop), and flying squirrels are among the specimens you might encounter here.

KEEP IN MIND

The zoo combines the breadth of a large museum and the terrain of a moderate hiking trail, so pace yourselves and keep expectations modest about how much you can cover. To save little (and big) feet, take the shuttle between Wild Asia and Zoo Center.

MAKE THE MOST OF YOUR TIME

The subway from Brooklyn and Manhattan takes at least 60 minutes to get here. But taking an express bus usually takes no more than 30. The BxM11 express bus stops along Madison Avenue, between 26th and 99th Streets, then travels directly to the Zoo's Bronx River entrance (Gate B). For your return trip, pick up the bus just outside the same gate at the MTA BxM11 sign (just before the underpass). Also bear in mind that Wednesday is a suggested donation day, so crowds may be especially dense in spring and summer.

Bronx River Pkwy. and
Fordham Rd., Bronx
Subway: 2 to Pelham Parkway

718/367-1010;
www.bronxzoo.com

$17 ages 13 and up, $12
children 3–12; rates change
seasonally; rides, attractions
and some special exhibits extra

Apr–Oct, M–F 10–5, Sa–Su and
holidays 10–5:30; Nov–Mar, daily
10–4:30; Children's Zoo Apr–Oct

1 and up, Children's Zoo
8 and under

You might also plan your route around some of the special attractions (all with separate admission fees unless you purchase a Total Experience ticket). These include the Bug Carousel, where insects substitute for horses; the Congo Gorilla Forest, with 20 lowland gorillas so remarkably human-like they often interact with visitors; the Wild Asia Monorail, showcasing elephants, rhinoceros, and tigers; as well as the Butterfly Garden, Children's Zoo, and Jungle World.

Family programs and activities are numerous, including Sea Lion Feedings, Primate Training, and Tiger Enrichment. But the biggest attraction is the Family Overnight Safari: After meeting some nocturnal creatures and doing zoo activities, kids five and older sleep in tents and wake up to the sound of peacocks. These sell out months in advance, so book the minute they become available.

If you like this sight, you may also like the Central Park Zoo (#56).

EATS FOR KIDS The food at the zoo has only gotten worse in recent years. Although there are several on-site cafés selling fries and heat-lamp burgers, we suggest bringing snacks and spreading out on the picnic tables, then venturing outside the zoo when dinner rolls around. If you're up for adventure, Arthur Avenue (aka The Bronx's Little Italy) is walking distance from the zoo. You can't go wrong at any of the restaurants lining this street, although local favorites seem to include **Dominick's** (2335 Arthur Ave., tel. 718/733–2807) and **Roberto's** (603 Crescent Ave., tel. 718/733–9503).

Although a botanical garden might be an enjoyable retreat for adults, kids could use your help to see it as more than just a collection of green things. To prep them properly, consider downloading the "Garden Exploration Activity Guide for Teachers" from the website's "School Visits" section.

This PDF guide helps families find avenues of approach to make the flora relevant to a kid's life. It is part conversation guide, part map, and it helps kids see how diverse and magnificent the plant world can be. It's also a great cheat sheet for organizing a family visit. The gardens can be done in any order, but the following are the can't-miss attractions.

The Children's Garden: The people who created this garden are all between three and 17. Your kids can join in the fun by planting crops and flowers under the guidance of instructors. There is also craft-making and imaginative play.

KEEP IN MIND Children under 12 are free here, and senior citizens are free on Friday year-round, so bring the grandparents. Saturday is also free 10–12 except on days when special public programs are scheduled. Mid-November through February is also a free for all, so if it's a mild day, consider checking out the garden as it prepares for winter.

990 Washington Ave., Brooklyn
Subway: 2, 3 to Eastern Parkway–Brooklyn
Museum; B (weekdays only), Q to Prospect Park;
4, 5 to Franklin Avenue; S to Prospect Park

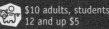 $10 adults, students
12 and up $5

 Mar–Oct, T–F 8–6, Sa–Su 10–6;
Nov–Mar, T–F 8–4:30, Sa–Su
10–4:30

 All ages

718/623-7200, 718/623-7333
program hotline; www.bbg.org

The Discovery Garden: Kids are invited to have interactive experiences with natural objects, such as touching and smelling plants, digging for worms, or journeying through various habitats (woodlands, meadow, farm, wetland).

Japanese Hill-and-Pond Garden. The wooden bridges and winding trails keep this garden visually interesting for kids and placid for parents.

Fragrance Garden: Have children close their eyes and smell their way around this garden, intentionally filled with plants that are recognizable by nose. Sniff your way around patchouli, lavender, peppermint, sage, basil, and more.

On Tuesdays and Thursdays there are free drop-in activities in the Discovery Garden. Summer visitors should check out the cool moonlit walk to explore bats and other nocturnal wildlife (6+).

If you like this sight, you may also like the New York Botanical Garden (#27).

EATS FOR KIDS Picnicking isn't allowed in the garden; however, the on-site **Terrace Café** does serve lunch outdoors from spring to early fall (meals are served in the Steinhardt Conservatory during late fall and winter). For deli sandwiches and its famous cheesecake, take a short ride to **Junior's Restaurant** (386 Flatbush Ave., tel. 718/852–5257), a classic '50s diner.

MAKE THE MOST OF YOUR TIME
If you can time your visit to co-incide with an autumn weekend, it's worth trying to attend one of the garden's free drop-in work-shops. They're held on selected Sundays in the fall.

Walking across the Brooklyn Bridge is not only a way to span—and experience—two boroughs, it's also a way to span two worlds. Looking at the cable pattern, stone towers, wood planks, and original toll prices (5¢ for a cow or horse, 2¢ for a hog or sheep) transports you back to the New York of the 1800s.

And looking at the Manhattan skyline, with its steeples of commerce practically hitting the heavens, is a reminder of its central role in today's society.

A classic NYC family experience is walking across the Brooklyn Bridge into Brooklyn, eating lunch at the Fulton Ferry Landing, then taking the Water Taxi back to South Street Seaport. Full of stunning vistas, this long walk definitely works up an appetite.

Once across the bridge, follow the path down the steps to Washington Street. Turn left on Front Street and again on Old Fulton Street, where you'll find a long line at

KEEP IN MIND

If you've run out of energy in Brooklyn, the F train will take you back to most places in Manhattan. Also, there are a few benches scattered along the bridge should you need to take a breather.

EATS FOR KIDS Fortify yourselves with a small chocolate at the amazing chocolatier **Jacques Torres** (66 Water St., tel. 718/875–9772) or a divine whoopie pie at **One Girl Cookies** (33 Main St., corner of Water, tel. 347/338–1268). Both shops open early, and rest assured that no one will judge you if you consume your treats at breakfast time.

Grimaldi's Pizza (19 Old Fulton St., tel. 718/858–4300). Arguably one of the best pizza places in the city, the wait is usually 30 minutes. After your meal, wander the neighborhood looking at the bookstores and boutiques. A highlight of your kids' visit will certainly be the homemade ice cream found in the pier-side former school house, the **Brooklyn Ice Cream Factory** (Old Fulton St., Brooklyn, tel. 718/246–3963). Take your scoops or sundae to the brand new Brooklyn Bridge Park, a lovely stretch of waterfront greenery, playgrounds, benches, and (in summer) water features and pool. Then, hop the Water Taxi to South Street Seaport to head back to Manhattan.

As an alternate route and shorter outing you might consider reversing your trek, taking the subway from Manhattan into Brooklyn (the A or C to High St., for instance), and walking the bridge back into Manhattan.

If you like this sight, you may also like the South Street Seaport Museum (#9).

MAKE THE MOST OF YOUR TIME The ideal
time to start this expedition is around 11 AM. This will give you plenty of time
to complete the walk and tour around. Alternatively, if you don't want to
do South Street Seaport, going around 5 PM in summer will set you up for a
gorgeous sunset from the pier before you leave. The walk itself is about 20
minutes with middle schoolers in tow, double that for toddlers or kids who
aren't accustomed to long strolls.

BROOKLYN CHILDREN'S MUSEUM

62

At first glance, the exhibits in this squat yellow building would only appear to yield an hour's worth of fun—which might have been the case if they weren't so interactive.

The main draw is, conveniently, one of the first things you'll encounter as you make your way inside: World Brooklyn, a 4,000-square-foot exhibit that replicates a streetscape of storefronts, highlighting the many vibrant cultures that call this borough home. You'll witness toddlers, 10-year-olds and all ages in between wordlessly becoming absorbed in their tasks, building a mock pizza with toppings or, in the case of the popular international grocery store, stocking shelves with all manner of goods and then ringing them up at cash registers. The play areas are also unusually roomy and clean, so parents can unobtrusively join in and not constantly reach for the hand sanitizer (though it's not a bad idea to do a quick wipe when you're through "shopping."

An unusual neon-lit tunnel (which kids are not *discouraged* from running through, if not necessarily encouraged) separates the streetscape from the museum's other areas,

KEEP IN MIND A visit to the nearby **Jewish Children's Museum** (792 Eastern Parkway, tel. 718/467–0600) will let your kids continue playing at a pretend Kosher Supermarket and Kitchen. Other hands-on exhibits celebrate Jewish holidays, biblical history, and the land of Israel.

145 Brooklyn Ave., Brooklyn
Subway: 3 to Kinston Ave.; A to Nostrand Ave.;
C to Kingston/Throop Ave.

 $9 per person

 T–Su 10–5

 9 and under

718/735–4400;
www.brooklynkids.org

including a sand-and-water playspace for tots and a nature exhibit with flowing water irresistible to splashy hands. Don't miss the small science inquiry center; there are quiet opportunities here to draw at individual desks or identify various animal x-rays after slapping them on to a light panel, the way doctors do. Somewhat inscrutably, this room is also home to Fantasia, a huge Burmese python and the museum's de facto mascot. (Fuzzy yellow Pythons and the like are available on-site in a gift shop heavy on science and nature toys.)

The museum's second floor is a bright, airy delight given over to temporary exhibits that in the past have included an interactive overview of international footwear and a historical selection of lunchboxes, which kids might be interested to know used to lean more toward raised metal (and cheesy-TV-show themes) rather than today's generic plastic.

If you like this sight, you may also like the Children's Museum of Manhattan (#55).

MAKE THE MOST OF YOUR TIME
Before you venture into the exhibition area, check out the information board for the day's programs. Offerings might include educator-led demonstrations at the museum's touch tank or greenhouse.

EATS FOR KIDS Visit the new **Kids Café** in the museum, which also opens onto the rooftop terrace for outdoor dining in good weather. Relatively healthy high-protein sandwiches are available along with hot dogs and vending machine fare. Note that shrewd local families frequently can be seen bringing in their own groceries for picnicking (which, like running in the neon tunnel, is not discouraged). A short walk away, **Eastern Chinese** (127 Kingston Ave., tel. 718/735–3408) serves Szechuan, Hunan, and Cantonese family favorites.

BROOKLYN MUSEUM

You'll notice that this museum's name is not followed by "of art." That's intentional—and good news for kids. Although it is grand in size (560,000 square feet), age (200+ years), and scope, the focus is firmly on inclusion.

The entrance—a relatively new addition, resembling a glass UFO that landed at the base of the gigantic neoclassical stone building—is a hint of the museum's fresh and welcoming attitude toward visitors of all ages.

Begin on the third floor with its way cool collection of Egyptian artifacts (aka mummies). After that, check out the current exhibits. Usually they're visually stimulating enough to appeal to kids. Recent ones have showcased Murakami, an anime-influenced artist who creates action-figure-like sculptures with bold colors and super-size features; a photographic collection of rock musicians; and a survey of the best of the Museum of Modern Art's Costume Collection (imagine 80 mannequins sporting chic dresses, pants, frilly shoes, and period hats).

EATS FOR KIDS

The **Museum Café** is open almost as long as the museum. **Tom's Restaurant** (782 Washington Ave., tel. 718 636–9738) is a quick walk away: It's a neighborhood institution that serves loads of kid-friendly fare.

MAKE THE MOST OF YOUR TIME

The museum is part of the Heart of Brooklyn initiative, which links some of the borough's best attractions. Literally next door are the Brooklyn Botanic Garden (#64), the main branch of the Brooklyn Public Library, and Prospect Park and its zoo (#20 and #19). A few blocks away is the Brooklyn Children's Museum (#62). Kids will tolerate a max of two to three hours here, so plan on spending the rest of your day running around outdoors or doing the Children's Museum.

200 Eastern Pkwy., Brooklyn
Subway: 2, 3 to Eastern Parkway/
Brooklyn Museum

Suggested donation $12 adults,
$8 students 12 and up

F–Su 11–6, W 11–6, Th 11–10,
1st Sa of month 5–11

718/638-5000;
www.brooklynmuseum.org

6 and up

If you still have their attention, take the kids to the Elizabeth A. Sackler Center for Feminist Art. Since the center's specific political and socio-cultural underpinnings will be lost on children under 10, stick with a simple message that most museums don't have many pieces of art by women. Kick off a conversation about women artists: "Have we seen any pictures on this trip made by women? Are there any famous female artists?" Then, point out how this is one of the few places where art by women has a home.

The Arts of Africa and Pacific Islands collections display objects with overly large limbs or heads and extreme facial expressions that amuse kids. Figures—such as the one from the Nicobar Islands or the monkey for Mbra—are like other cultures' Polly Pockets.

If you like this sight, you may also like the Museum of Modern Art (#34).

KEEP IN MIND Don't just make a day of it. Make a night of it! The Museum's premier event for all ages, First Saturdays, takes place from 5 to 11 every month except September. This family-friendly event is free, and features music in the galleries, art-making projects, films, performances, and gallery talks. A dance party that feels like a giant block party ends it with a bang. Flat-rate parking is a bargain after 5, and the **Museum Café** stays open so you can enjoy dinner with the family.

CARL SCHURZ PARK

If you only have time to visit one park in New York City, most of the eight million people who live here will likely direct you to Central Park, though you'll run into plenty of diehard Prospect Park (#20) fans as well as champions of Riverside Park (part of the Greenway Bike/Walking Path, #46).

Ask Upper East Siders specifically what one you must see, and they'll still tell you Central Park. Why? In part because it's the majority answer, but it's also because they want Carl Schurz Park to keep its "well-kept secret" status.

For the full-on Carl Schurz local experience, enter the park at 88th St. and East End, pointing out to your kids the quaint Federal-style wood-frame house to your left. "That's Gracie Mansion, where the mayor is allowed to live," you might say. "Who cares," your kid may say back.

In any event, apathy about the landmark will dissipate as you continue toward the East River and reach the promenade, which is treasured by local parents as a continuous and

KEEP IN MIND During the year, the Carl Schurz Park Conservancy organizes free musical and artistic programs. It also hosts a popular harvest festival in mid-October, when kids are delighted to discover that a pumpkin patch has magically appeared in the park. Check the website for a schedule of children's activities.

East End Ave. to the East River,
E.84th to E.90th Sts.
Subway: 4, 5, 6 to 86th St.

 Free

 Daily, dawn–1AM

 212/459–4455; www.
carlschurzparknyc.org

1 and up

(relatively) even concrete path where their kids can ride bikes or scooters or simply run like crazy.

Speaking of running, the dog runs at 86th Street are a favorite local haunt for dog owners and dog watchers. If you come on a nice day—and you should—owners will be out in force exercising their canines in the runs (one for smaller dogs toward the front of the promenade, and a lesser-used one for bigger dogs to the side). The energy of the dogs will likely please your young ones—and perhaps provoke them to ask you if they can get a puppy of their own.

Your park tour ends at 84th St, where the Catbird Playground awaits with swings (often unoccupied ones!) and an elevated play structure with the requisite slides and ladders for the kids, plus plenty of benches for you if you want to take a minute to congratulate yourself for finding your way here.

If you like this sight, you may also like the High Line (#43).

MAKE THE MOST OF YOUR TIME

If you're going to be anywhere in the vicinity of the Museum Mile—and perhaps visiting a museum—bringing a picnic lunch here afterwards is a nice idea.

EATS FOR KIDS In keeping with the whole picnic-in-the-park concept, one of the better and more enduring places to pick up sandwiches and salads is **Tal's Bagels** (333 East 86th St., tel. 212/427–6811). For excellent fish tacos, chicken quesadillas, and crunchy free vegetable chips right when you sit down, try **Cilantro** (1712 2nd Avenue at 89th St., tel. 212/722–4242), a popular neighborhood spot that will be uncrowded if you go on a weekday afternoon.

CARNEGIE HALL

How do you get to Carnegie Hall? Practice . . . practice . . . or just attend one of the family concerts held weekend afternoons throughout the year on this world-famous stage and in Zankel Hall, located underneath the main hall.

The popular family concert series, which began here in 1995, introduces children to classical, jazz, and folk music at affordable, family-friendly prices. Pre-concert activities on the main stage and in other smaller Carnegie Hall spaces include storytelling, hands-on musical experiences, and instrument demonstrations.

Another noteworthy program, McGraw-Hill CarnegieKids concerts are free and, with a running time of 45 minutes, designed for the attention span of preschoolers. These concerts are not held in the main hall, however, but rather in the Kaplan space on the fifth floor.

MAKE THE MOST OF YOUR TIME

At select performances, usually excluding the family concert series, you can buy partial-view seats for $10 from noon until one hour before showtime (limit two tickets per patron; first come, first served). Also, select performances sell student and senior tickets for $10 during the same time frame.

KEEP IN MIND Can't get to Carnegie Hall? Let Carnegie Hall come to you. Since 1976, the Neighborhood Concert Series (a program of the Weill Music Institute at Carnegie Hall) has hosted free one-hour concerts in libraries, community and senior centers, and shelters in all five boroughs. This is a great way to experience concerts in a small venue without dressing to the nines or paying a high price (or any price for that matter). Individual artists and ensembles perform repertoires from classical to pop each season. Best of all, some concerts are Workshop Concerts or Kids Concerts. Seating is first come, first served.

154 W. 57th St., at 7th Ave.
Subway: 1, A, C, B, D to 59th St./Columbus
Circle; N, Q, R to 57th St./7th Ave

 Family concerts $9;
tour $10 adults,
$8 students,
$4 under 12

 Tours daily in concert season,
performances permitting

212/247-7800, 212/903-9765 tour
updates; www.carnegiehall.org

 Family concerts 5 and up,
McGraw-Hill Carnegiekids
3-6, tour 7 and up

One-hour guided tours of the venue are also given. And if your kids want to get a close-up look at Benny Goodman's clarinet or catch a glimpse of Arturo Toscanini's baton, they can do so by visiting the second-floor Rose Museum: It's open daily 11–4:30 during the concert season as well as to concert patrons in the evening. East of the main auditorium, this small museum displays interesting mementos from Carnegie Hall's rich history, and admission is free.

If you like this sight you may also like Symphony Space (#6).

EATS FOR KIDS Before a concert or at intermission, visit the **Citi Café,** on the Parquet level, for light fare or desserts. The **Zankel Hall Bar** outside the auditorium also has light fare and drinks. Alternately, head over to **Brooklyn Diner** (212 W. 57th St., tel. 212/581–8900) for generous portions of well-prepared comfort foods and decadent desserts. You can order the quintessential corned beef on rye and bowl of matzoh ball soup at the **Carnegie Deli** (854 7th Ave., tel. 212/757–2245) as long as you bring plenty of cash (no credit cards accepted) and a good appetite.

CATHEDRAL CHURCH OF ST. JOHN THE DIVINE

Regardless of your religious affiliation, you gotta love a place in the middle of Manhattan that's so big the Statue of Liberty could fit under the dome. (At 121,000 square feet, it qualifies as the world's largest cathedral.)

A walk around the exterior will get imaginations spinning, thanks to some pretty funky architectural elements. In addition to the usual creepy gargoyles, species-confused animals, and saints and martyrs with no eyes, there are some figures that are simply baffling. The workman with hard hat and measuring tape; Hamlet holding poor Yorick's skull; a baby's head emerging from a flower? All things weird and wonderful.

A walk around inside reinforces the church's inclusive motto, "A House of Prayer for All People." Each of its chapels is dedicated to a different national, ethnic, or social group, including The American Poet's Corner (where 30 writers have been inducted including Walt Whitman, Emily Dickinson, and Robert Frost), the FDNY memorial (originally commemorating firefighters killed in a 1966 fire but now expanded to be a tribute to 9/11 heroes), and

KEEP IN MIND Check the calendar for seasonal events, the Blessing of the Animals (in October) being by far the most popular. In the past zebras, elephants, and, of course, thousands of NYC pets have been blessed here. The Blessing of the Bikes in April is similar but far less fluffy. And the Procession of the Ghouls (NOT for young children or those easily scared) may be the most bizarre Halloween event to take place inside any church. Typically, this is followed by a screening of the silent film *Nosferatu* accompanied by a church organ.

1047 Amsterdam Ave.
Subway: 1, 9 to Cathedral Parkway

212/316–7540, 212/932–7347 tour
information; www.stjohndivine.org

 Free, suggested donation for
Highlight Tours $8, Vertical
Tours $15, $12 student

Daily 7–6

4 and up, 8 and up for
most tours or workshops

the St. Savior's chapel (honoring Christian communities of the East, it includes two Buddhist temple cabinets to honor Asians as well).

In terms of guided tours, there are several to pick from. The Highlight Tour is free (fees are merely suggested) and touches on, well, church highlights. It lasts about an hour, but it's not unusual to break off when you'd rather tool around on your own. Adults and kids 12 or older can also participate in the Vertical Tour. On this one, you climb 124 feet via a spiral staircase, learning about the sanctuary's art and architecture along the way. At the top, a magnificent view of Manhattan awaits.

Prefer a hands-on approach? On Saturdays do one of the nature- or medieval-based workshops. Recent ones have included Stained Glass, Medieval Arts (such as designing gargoyles), and Wonders of the Sun (making sundials).

If you like this sight, you may also like the Rubin Museum (#12).

MAKE THE MOST OF YOUR TIME

Call to make workshop reservations in advance, as they can fill up quickly, especially in winter. On warm days, the peace-themed children's sculpture garden is a divine place to just kick back.

EATS FOR KIDS When a sweet treat is in order, hit the **Hungarian Pastry Shop** (1030 Amsterdam Ave., tel. 212/866–4230). A neighborhood institution for a zillion years, it's pretty much frozen in time, from the menu (painted on upper cabinets and never changed) to the specialities (baklava, strudels, cookies) to the cash-only policy. For healthier fare, pop into **Whole Foods** (808 Columbus Ave., tel. 212/222–6160) and cobble together fresh fixings for a picnic for the Cathedral grounds.

CENTRAL PARK

57

You could spend an entire vacation in Central Park without taking advantage of all this enormous urban refuge has to offer.

The southernmost square mile, after all, contains attractions that could easily be stand-alone all-day activities—namely Central Park Zoo (#56) and Wollman Rink, which in summer morphs into the Victorian Gardens amusement park (#3). Start from one of these (the Zoo is a good bet) and move on from there.

Favorite peaceful pursuits include catching a show at the Swedish Cottage Marionette Theater (advance reservations required, 79th St. Transverse, tel. 212/988–9093), renting model sailboats on the Conservatory Water (a pond which might look familiar from the boat race scene in *Stuart Little*), and walking upstairs at Belvedere Castle (79th St. Transverse, tel. 212/772–0210) to drink in the view.

One glorious spot that's often overlooked, even by locals, is the Conservatory Garden at 105th St. and Fifth Avenue. The park's only formal garden has lush, diligently manicured English, French, and Italian gardens; and although it's a designated quiet area, you

KEEP IN MIND

No tax dollars go toward the park's upkeep. So becoming a member of The Central Park Conservancy is a way to show your appreciation (the website has details). Joining is also good way to get discounts at area hotels, eateries, and attractions like Victorian Gardens (#3).

MAKE THE MOST OF YOUR TIME Newcomers spend more time trying to figure out how to get between places than actually enjoying them, and while it isn't a bad idea to get a park map—either in advance or at the Dairy Visitor Center and Gift Shop (65th St., mid-park, tel. 212/794–6564)—it's not entirely necessary, as the park has upped its posted visual map signs in recent years and you can always harass a passing jogger for directions.

Bordered by 5th Ave., Central Park West, 59th St., and 110th St.
Subway: Dairy Visitor Center, 6 to 66th St.

 Free; some attractions charge

Daily sunrise–sunset

212/360-3444;
www.centralparknyc.org

 All ages

shouldn't let that dissuade you from taking reasonably well-behaved kids in. Since you'll be at the park's northern end anyway, this is a good opportunity for wintertime visitors to try out the Lasker Rink, an underappreciated stepchild of Wollman Rink to the south.

Of the 20+ playgrounds in and around Central Park, Hecksher is the most magnificent, with castle towers and a moat (when it's over 80°F, sprinklers and "rivers" run through); a giant sandbox with a climbing web, tunnels, and swings; two AstroTurf picnic areas; slides; swings; and four recently built clean bathrooms.

A small path away, the 1903 Friedsam Memorial Carousel (Center Dr. and 65th St.) is adorned with some of the world's largest hand-carved horses.

As you meander, allow time for kids to climb sculptures (especially Balto the dog and Alice in Wonderland), watch buskers, climb rocks, lounge in the Sheep Meadow, or just people-watch.

If you like this sight, you may also like Prospect Park (#20).

EATS FOR KIDS The **Boathouse** restaurant has lovely views of the lake and equally lovely food, but requires advance reservations and is definitely not for young kids. Luckily, you can get practically the same view with a more chaotic kid-friendly atmosphere at **The Boathouse Café** (tel. 212/517–2233). For the ideal picnic, head to the Sheep Meadow. Sandwiches, drinks and other supplies can be purchased in delis along Broadway, Amsterdam, and Columbus Avenues; don't wait until you get to Central Park West to buy grab-and-go food, as you won't find it easily or inexpensively.

CENTRAL PARK ZOO

Mercifully compact for a big-city zoo, this 7-acre oasis for creatures great and small is easy enough to knock off in a couple hours, barring congestion from local regulars and school groups.

That said, unless you want to feel caged, come early-afternoon on a weekday, when the number of visitors has thinned out. The monkeys, polar bears, penguins, tropical birds, and seals are among the most popular residents, so if you do detect a heavy class-trip presence the day you arrive, know that these areas will be especially crowded,

Watching the sea lion feeding is a little anticlimactic, but the anticipation is almost obligatory. Get to the sea lion area at least 20 minutes early to snag a spot up against the railing on the north side of the tank, where the handlers dole out fish. (Check the website for updated feeding times.) Along the way to the polar bears, look at the snow leopard exhibit, head down the steps to be inches away from a polar bear, and then chill out in

KEEP IN MIND While you won't find creatures within the zoo as whimsical as the ones in *Madagascar*, the instrument-playing bronze animals atop the Delacorte Music Clock (near the Children's Zoo entrance) come close. Every half hour, a horn-blowing kangaroo, a pipe-tooting goat, a violin-playing hippo and a penguin on drums knock out children's songs, picking from a playlist of 44 tunes throughout the year.

Central Park at 64th St. and 5th Ave.
Subway: 5 to 68th St./Hunter College;
N, R, W to 5th Ave./59th St.

 212/439-6500;
www.centralparkzoo.org

 $12 ages 13
and up, $7
children 3–12

 Late Mar–early May, M–Fr 10–5, Sa–Su
10–5:30; late May–early Sept, daily 10–5:30;
early Sept–early Nov, M–Fr 10–5, Sa–Su
10–5:30; early Nov–late Mar, daily 10–5

 All ages

the penguin house, which, like most penguin houses, smells like penguin. Kids can generally overlook this, though—especially if you're lifting the smaller ones up to get better views of these engaging flightless creatures.

The Rain Forest brings the tropics indoors. With jungle plants, waterfalls, and colorful birds, kids will happily spend 20 minutes or more in here.

Visit the Tisch Children's Zoo with children nine and under. A combo petting zoo and playspace, this spot contains a few kid-friendly farm animals (bring quarters to buy food); photo ops like big bunny cutouts; and a well-designed climbing web where kids get their wiggles out while balancing on rope.

If you like this sight, you may also like the Prospect Park Zoo (#19).

EATS FOR KIDS

The once outstanding on-site café is now best avoided. Instead, for a breakfast/brunch/anytime treat, go to **Norma's** in the Parker Meriden (188 W. 57th St., tel. 212/708–7460) for decadently sweet waffles and pancakes, eggs, burgers, and other tasty comfort foods.

MAKE THE MOST OF YOUR TIME Combined with a
visit to the Tisch Children's Zoo, this is easily a three- to four-hour adventure, even for restless kids. Since your admission price gets you into both places, you may want to break your visit into two. Start with the highlights at the main zoo, then let kids feed the animals and play on the climbing structures at the kids' zoo. Head back to the main zoo when the crowds dwindle to do the more subtle attractions like the red panda.

CHILDREN'S MUSEUM OF MANHATTAN

CMOM (as its known to locals) is a victory in playrooms for the people. Although it far prefers to see itself as a museum that educates and increases awareness of other cultures, it is, in essence, a giant indoor playground.

The third-floor PlayWorks is a mixed-use play area, though it's dominated by kids six and under blowing off steam. You'll find climbable platforms, a pretend fire truck and MTA bus, plus a store area with plastic groceries to shelve and check out. There's also a small, soft toddler area with some interactive displays as well as a popular (and messy) paint wall for finger-painting.

The second-most-popular spot, Adventures with Dora and Diego, is geared toward toddlers and preschoolers and branded with depictions of the titular Nickelodeon characters. As you enter there's a cluster of rain-forest trees, a musical instrument area, a wooden footbridge, and other accoutrements of Dora's world. Unlike the Playworks open floor plan, the Dora area is more linear and cramped, so that when it does get crowded, it's a challenge for parents to stay out of each other's way.

KEEP IN MIND

So much to do, so little time? Leave the stroller at home or in the car, and avoid the long lines at the coat/stroller check.

EATS FOR KIDS

An enduring Upper West Side eatery that's pretty consistent with quick service and generous portions, **Arties Delicatessen** (2290 Broadway at 83rd St., tel. 212/579–5959) has above-average deli sandwiches, hot dogs, and soups. Food is not allowed inside the museum, so if you want to try picnicking consider grabbing bagels and cheeses or handy pre-prepared salads and spreads from **Zabar's** (2245 Broadway, tel. 212/787–2000) and either head to the Tecumseh Playground (Amsterdam Ave./77th St.) or duck into the West Side Community Garden (123 W. 89th St.), a serene block-long spot with greenery, flowers, and benches.

Tisch Building, 212 W. 83rd St.
Subway: 1 to 79th St.; B (weekdays),
C to 81st St.

 $11 ages 1 and up; free
1st Fri of month 5–8

 T–F and Su 10–5, Sa 10–7

212/721–1234; www.cmom.org

Infant–8

The ground floor has rotating exhibits. Although these are thoughtfully conceived and executed, most kids judge them by playground standards. For example, an Ancient Greece exhibit was educational but not great fun, whereas an exhibit geared toward healthier lifestyles was more successful thanks to its amusing crawl-through digestive system. As with any large playspace, it can be a challenge to track kids when it gets crowded, so be sure to stick by your younger kids while here.

CMOM's most delightful feature is typically open in summer, as it is outside and down some steps in a partially covered play area: City Splash invites young visitors to explore the physical properties of water as they splash and float toy boats along pretend waterways. For everyone's sake, smocks are provided.

If you like this sight, you may also like the Brooklyn Children's Museum (#62).

MAKE THE MOST OF YOUR TIME Public pro-
grams geared toward the under-four and over-five sets are held on the top floor.
Check on arrival to see if there's one you want to join. (Art and craft classes
are the most handy when you're with kids of mixed ages.) Leave ample time to
get your kids into the elevator or up the stairs for the program before it starts.

CHILDREN'S MUSEUM OF THE ARTS

54

Formerly occupying a genuinely artsy but somewhat cramped and confining space, this museum has moved about a mile from its old location into a bigger facility that does justice to the spectacular programs and staff.

It is anchored by a central 2,000-square-foot gallery space that rotates exhibits several times a year to spotlight visual artists: The inaugural one in this space in 2011 celebrated artists who take pains to make their work available to the public, such as Keith Haring and Christo & Jeanne-Claude (of the orange gates of Central Park fame).

Likewise, the museum also rotates out parts of a permanent 2,000-piece collection composed of drawings and paintings made by children. Their creativity is truly the focus here, as various studios flanking the main gallery are dedicated to making and appreciating art and music. Particularly popular is the Clay Bar stocked with clay and other art materials. Like most of the activities here, clay play is overseen by teaching artists (practicing artists

MAKE THE MOST OF YOUR TIME Kids wanting to pony up to the Clay Bar must sign up first. Do this upon arrival so that you can explore other parts of the museum while you're waiting for your designated time slot.

103 Charlton St.
Subway: 1 to Houston St.;
B, D, F, A, C, E to West 4th

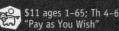 $11 ages 1–65; Th 4–6
"Pay as You Wish"

M, W and Sa–Su 10–5,
Th–F 12–6

 212/274-0986; www.cmany.org

 1–10

who have serious kid-people skills). Their talents are particularly welcome in the WEE Arts Studio, where the teaching artists supervise music and art activities and do story time with the one-to-five set. Note that, for part of the week, the studio holds drop-in classes for an extra fee. But it dedicates several hours a day to those paying general admission beginning at noon on weekdays and at 10 on weekends.

For older children (and grown-ups), teaching artists oversee workshops in a media lab, where films and animations created on-site will find their way onto the museum's blog. To extend the idea of art by and for kids into other media, there are 10 listening stations where you can hear music created by kids (and some professional musicians, too).

If you like this sight, you may also like the Museum of the Moving Image (#32).

KEEP IN MIND In recent years CMA has partnered with Governor's Island (#47) to bring art and art activities to the island during summer weekends and also to screen and display artwork created by children in the museum's media lab.

EATS FOR KIDS Grab muffins and decent premade sandwiches or salads at **Hudson Coffee Bar** (350 Hudson St., bet. Charlton and King, tel. 212/727-8885). For more of a sit-down, **P.J. Charlton Italian Restaurant** (549 Greenwich St., tel. 212/243-9831) has pastas and chicken parm as well as good burgers.

CIRCLE LINE SIGHTSEEING CRUISES

If you've been on one tour cruise, you've been on them all. Right? Well, you can test this hypothesis by shutting your eyes when you embark on a ride with Circle Line.

You'll notice that the rush of the ocean will sound the way it did the last time you took a boat ride. The motion of the ship will seem about the same. There will be no discernible difference in how the chilly air feels on deck or how the stuffy air feels in the cabin. And the salty, wet air will smell as it always does.

Now open your eyes. If you're aboard the Circle Line, you'll see what the difference is.

The view of Manhattan from the deck of a ship is singular and spectacular, whether you're doing the full three-hour, 360° circle tour of the island or just the semicircle, which hugs the bottom part of Lower Manhattan, semi-circling once and then doubling back so that passengers on the other side of the boat can snap their photos without switching sides.

KEEP IN MIND

If a cruise sounds too languorous, consider the Circle Line's amped-up option: The Beast, a half-hour speedboat ride that runs you over to the Statue of Liberty and back. May through September, it departs every hour on the half hour between 10 and 6. Riders must be at least 40" tall.

MAKE THE MOST OF YOUR TIME
While the full-circle cruise is only a few bucks more than the semi, it is a full hour longer—and that will feel like one of the longest hours of your life if you're with a child under four, especially if the weather doesn't cooperate and you're stuck inside the cabin for a while. So with little ones consider choosing the semicircle tour. It will give them a more-than-adequate cruise experience.

Pier 83, West 42nd St. and 12th Ave. Subway: 1, 2, 3, A, C, E, N, Q, R to Times Sq./42nd St.

212/563-3200; www.circleline42.com

Circle (full island) cruise $38 adults, $25 children 3–12; semicircle $34 adults, $23 children 3–12

Circle cruise Jan–mid-Mar 2:30, mid-Mar–Apr 11:30, 3; late Apr–Oct 10, 12:30, 3:30; late Oct–Dec 12:30; semicircle and other cruise times vary

3 and up

On the semicircle tour, in other words, you only see points of interest on the lower portion of the island, including Ellis Island and the Statue of Liberty, South Street Seaport, and the *Intrepid*. The advantage of the full circle is that you can ogle the northern tip of the island from the water, which is a view you seldom get.

A tour guide will deliver fun factoids about landmarks you know, as well as about ones you don't. For instance, The Octagon, now a high-end apartment building on Roosevelt Island, was the administrative building of a mental hospital in the mid-1800s (though back then it went by the un-PC term "lunatic asylum"). The tour guide will talk too much—as they all tend to do for fear you think you're not getting your money's worth—but during the silences, wordlessly take in the view, and encourage your kids to do the same.

If you like this sight, you may also like the Greenway Bike/Walking Path (#46).

EATS FOR KIDS You're permitted to bring your own food and soft drinks on to the boat (booze and snacks are sold onboard), and that's the best idea no matter which tour you take. If you've done an afternoon sail, however, and want to tuck into an early dinner, head over to **Lucky Strike** (624–660 W 42nd St., between 11th and 12th Aves., tel. 646/829–0170). After bowling a few frames, you can enjoy above-average burgers and sandwiches or unexpected bowling alley fare like short ribs and salmon.

CONEY ISLAND

52

"**S**tep Right Up! See a fire-breathing woman swallow torches right before your eyes!" Yes, you will actually hear carnival barkers here, and that's all a part of the nostalgic fun. Coney Island may no longer be able to outshine big-league amusement parks, but it's still an absolute kids' favorite.

Begin with Luna Park. In addition to the requisite midway games, it has 19 rides that range from mild to intense. One standout among the latter is Air Race, an airplane thrill that subjects bodies to 4Gs of force as it vertically spins them 360 degrees. Family rides for younger folk and 'fraidy cats are positioned closer to the Boardwalk.

Spend the hottest part of the day at the beach, or visit the Aquarium to escape the midday sun. In the afternoon, stroll the Boardwalk and play in the playground on the way to a Brooklyn Cyclones baseball game (tel. 718/449-8497; www.brooklyncyclones.com). This talented minor-league team is just part of the attraction: Kids can also experience face painting, cheerleaders, magicians, raffles, T-shirt giveaways, ball tosses, fireworks, and base running.

KEEP IN MIND Luna Park may be the newest amusement area, but Deno's has the highest and one of the oldest rides: The Wonder Wheel, which gives great views of the ocean, the Manhattan Skyline, and Coney Island. It has only stopped once in its 90-year history (on July 13, 1977, during the Great NYC Blackout). Younger kids should stick to the stationary cars. And, of course, the Cyclone, a nostalgic wood rollercoaster, can still give a plunging thrill that competes with modern hydraulic giants.

Southern tip of Brooklyn
Subway: Q, F to West 8th St.; D, F, N, Q
to Coney Island-Stillwell Ave.

 Free; amusement
park rides vary

 Attraction hrs vary
by season

718/802–3846 Brooklyn Tourism and Visitors
Center, 718/372–5159 Coney Island USA;
www.visitbrooklyn.org, www.coneyisland.com

1 and up

Lively traditional circus sideshows, complete with a fire-eater, sword swallower, snake charmer, and contortionist, are featured at Sideshows by the Seashore (W. 12th St. and Surf Ave., tel. 718/372–5159), the last-standing 10-in-1 sideshow in the country. Sideshows generally begin in the spring and have a finite season, so call ahead to confirm the hours. Upstairs from the sideshows, you can find the Coney Island Museum (open Friday–Sunday noon to 5), which contains exhibits spotlighting historic Coney Island and related memorabilia. An extensive array of tourist information and literature is also available here. Before leaving, make your Coney Island day complete by eating at Nathan's and getting a candy apple or taffy from William's Candy Shop—neither of which look much different than when they opened in the first half of the last century.

If you like this sight, you may also like Victorian Gardens (#3).

MAKE THE MOST OF YOUR TIME

Like a carnival, Coney Island is an in-season venue. In summer the rides are open, the beach has lifeguards, and the whole place hums. Leave the watch at home and expect to spend at least six hours having a ball here.

EATS FOR KIDS Make the 60-minute subway ride go faster by bringing a nutritious snack to eat on the train. It'll help balance the avalanche of sweets to come. When you arrive, the boardwalk is bursting with crinkle fries, cotton candy, funnel cakes, Italian ices, and candy apples. Gorging on them is all part of the experience. You'll be hard-pressed to find a true sit-down dining option without venturing off the main drag to Brighton Beach, unless you want pizza at **Totonno's** (1524 Neptune Ave., between W. 15th and W. 16th, tel. 718/372–8606).

EL MUSEO DEL BARRIO

At El Museum del Barrio's grand reopening in 2009, the CEO described how the building's masonry was replaced by glass so that the city's light could shine in while the energy of El Museo shines out, and you may feel a little boost when you gaze at it.

Rafael Montañez Ortiz founded the museum in 1969 to reflect the Latino cultural experience, which at the time wasn't represented in NYC's mainstream museums. And it does a wonderful job of connecting a disparate community through Puerto Rican, Caribbean, and Latin American art. If that sounds serious, don't worry. Even kids too young to understand this political and cultural context will naturally be drawn to the bright colors and tangible folk art.

The permanent collection contains 6,500 objects representing over 800 years of Latino history and culture through prints, drawings, paintings, sculptures, photographs, film, video, works on paper, and artifacts. Young visitors will enjoy the dolls, animal figures,

KEEP IN MIND

For a quiet stroll or calming break in your touring, dip into Central Park's Conservatory Garden (#57). This tranquil retreat is located nearby.

EATS FOR KIDS Stay at the museum and eat at **El Café** to get regional specialties like chilled tomato soup with cilantro or *arepa con carne*. To fully immerse kids in the Latino experience, try tapas and Puerto Rican specialties at **Camaradasel Barrio Bar and Restaurant** (2241 1st Ave. at 115th, tel. 212/348–2703).

1230 5th Ave.
Subway: 6 to 103rd St.; 2, 3 to
110th St. and Lenox Ave.

212/831-7272; www.elmuseo.org

$9 ages 13 and up, $5 students;
free under 12 on W, free every
3rd Sa 11-6

T-Sa 11-6, Su 1-5

5 and up

the fur baseball glove, and other whimsical items. Older kids may particularly like the works on paper, or the paintings and sculptures. A favorite piece of eye-catching color and energy is *La Cama,* a sculpture of an ornate bed by Pepon Osorio. Signage throughout the museum is in Spanish and English.

During Target Free Third Saturdays the museum not only throws open its doors but also holds concerts, screenings, and workshops. Other popular events include the Three Kings Day Parade in January: Students and organizations may register to march in it, and everyone is welcome to come watch the pageantry. In June the museum is a major stop in Manhattan's Museum Mile event, with free admission to view the current exhibitions, as well as live music and dancing.

If you like this sight, you may also like the Rubin Museum (#12).

MAKE THE MOST OF YOUR TIME A visit here should take about two hours, leaving plenty of time to catch a Children's Read Aloud program at the Aguilar Branch of the New York Public Library (174 E. 110th St., tel. 212/534-2930) or one of the other kids' events frequently scheduled there. Also close by is the Guggenheim (#44).

ELLIS ISLAND

If you are an American citizen, there's a 50-50 chance you are descended from one of the immigrants who entered this country via Ellis Island. For parents who fit that criteria, explaining how your child is the great- or great-great grandchild of a specific passenger gives you the perfect way to begin framing a trip here.

Another way to engage kids, perhaps after you've gone through Castle Clinton and boarded the ferry, is to mention that of the 12 million immigrants who passed through Ellis Island, the very first was Annie Moore: a 15-year-old girl from Ireland who would end up having at least 11 children of her own and living the rest of her life as a New Yorker. Hers is one of many compelling stories that will unfold for your family as you tour the Registry Room (aka the Great Hall, where immigrants were processed) as well as the different exhibit galleries.

Doing the audio tour, which takes you through all of the galleries, is a must. Along the way, you'll absorb Ellis Island's significance through minutiae, like the diversity of foods

KEEP IN MIND If you're visiting during the warmer months (particularly on busy summer afternoons), try to purchase reserved ferry tickets ahead of time; you'll not only have your tickets but you'll wait in a shorter line once you get to the ferry terminal, too.

New York Harbor, ferry leaves from South Ferry in Battery Park
Subway: 4, 5 to Bowling Green; 1 to South Ferry; R, W to
Whitehall

 Free; ferry $17
ages 13 and up;
$9 children 4–12

 Daily 9:30–4:50, ferry
daily every 25 minutes;
closed Dec. 25

877/523-9849 tickets and monument passes,
212/363-3200 Ellis Island information;
www.statuecruises.com, www.nps.gov

7 and up

cooks needed to make, the baggage people brought, or the toys and games children played with. During the tour you'll also hear actual Ellis Island immigrants tell their own stories.

If you've never searched for a descendant, you can begin the process at home by perusing the online passenger records database at www.ellisisland.org. If you not only know you're descended from an immigrant but have also had that person's name etched on the island's spiraling metal Wall of Honor, you've got a great family activity ahead of you. Head out to the wall with a paper and pencil and have your child do a rubbing of his or her ancestor's name to take home. Just remember to pay your respects to the statue of Annie Moore before you leave.

If you like this sight, you may also like the Statue of Liberty (#7).

EATS FOR KIDS
The **Ellis Café** is a stellar example of what every attraction should have. There is a good selection of burgers, salads, sandwiches, and fish, and the eatery strives to include as many organic and healthy options as possible. Most are made fresh daily. On warm days, sit at the terrace tables for a great view of Lower Manhattan.

MAKE THE MOST OF YOUR TIME
The audio tour is de rigueur to make the proverbial walls talk. That means you should set aside at least three hours, including the round-trip ferry ride. Families with kids over 12 might want to consider combining this with a visit to the Statue of Liberty, but those with younger kids should stick with one attraction at a time. Unlike those for the Statue of Liberty, tickets for same-day Ellis Island ferry rides are easy to get (the monument is free, you only pay for the ride and the audio tour).

EMPIRE STATE BUILDING

From *Sleepless in Seattle* to *Gossip Girl*, movies and TV programs have built up the romance of this iconic building where characters race to the top for a fateful rendezvous. What none of those scenes show is the Byzantine process involved in actually reaching said observation deck—one that's far more arduous with a hot, tired, or hungry child in tow.

Yes, you come to experience one of the world's most amazing urban views, but you will spend 10 times longer getting there than seeing it. In other words, the *only* way to do this building with younger children is by bringing distractions and refreshments.

Rent the audio tour for everyone over six. Disregard the narrator's instruction to start it on the elevator. Begin listening immediately. As you make your way up, you'll learn the exciting history of the building's construction (the 1,454-foot-tall structure was built in a year and 45 days for $41 million) and the heated competition between it and the Chrysler Building to earn the coveted title of "world's tallest" building. The tour goes beyond

KEEP IN MIND

Top of the Rock at Rockefeller Center (#13), 10 blocks north, has an excellent view without the wait. Better yet, it delivers one thing the Empire State Building doesn't: a view the Empire State Building itself. You can buy timed-entry tickets online and on-site.

MAKE THE MOST OF YOUR TIME

There are five different lines to get to the 86th floor. The first is outdoors and the wait time can range from seconds to half an hour. The second, third, and fourth are all to buy tickets and get to the first elevator. The final line, winding around ropes on the 80th floor, is unfortunately the slowest. Buying an express pass ($47.50) is a worthwhile investment because it allows you to bypass all of these lines (except security) and get right to the top. Otherwise, go early in the morning (around 8) or early evening for smaller crowds.

350 5th Ave., at 34th St.
Subway: 1, 2, 3 to Penn Station/34th St.; B, D,
F, N, Q, R to 34th St/Avenue of the Americas

 $25 adults, $19 children
6–12; $47.50 express
ticket for all ages

Daily 8 AM–2 AM, last
elevator at 1:15 AM

 212/736-3100; www.esbnyc.com

 3 and up

facts and figures, giving a sociological spin to the icon. First-time New York visitors may want to buy the panoramic graphic ($5) showing all of the major buildings you can see from the top.

The view from the 86th-floor observatory is full-on magnificent (on a sunny day you can see 80 miles in all directions). The audio tour will point out most of the major landmarks familiar to kids from movies or TV (the Brooklyn Bridge, for instance) and then some. Unless money is no object, take a pass on the Skyride and the 102nd-floor observatory.

If you like this sight, you may also like Rockefeller Center and the Ice Rink (#13).

EATS FOR KIDS **Heartland Brewery** (350 5th Ave. at 34th St., tel. 212/563-3433) has a solid selection of comfort foods like mac-and-cheese, chicken and ribs, and fish-and-chips, plus beer (every now and then mom and dad really do need one!). Being as the Empire State Building borders the neighborhood known as Korea Town, you can also sample Korean BBQ and Udon noodles or perhaps some more adventurous savories at **New Wonjo Restaurant** (23 West 32nd Street, tel. 212/695-5815).

F.A.O. SCHWARZ

Before the toy-soldier doorman permits your family to enter this most beloved of New York retail stores, know two things. First, like the nearby Apple Store, F.A.O. is visually arresting, and that's a good reason to visit. Second, just as it's okay to take a pass on that iPad your kids keep hinting about at the Apple Store, it's okay to leave F.A.O. without purchasing any of the high-priced toys they may have longingly carried around.

Now you can go in.

Once through the main Fifth Avenue entrance, you'll be immersed in the huge-stuffed-animal section. Life-size giraffes, 8-foot grizzlies, 5-foot zebras, lions, and polar bears all populate this area. Next, ride up to the second floor to jump on the oversize keyboard that your kids may or may not recognize from a pivotal scene in the movie *Big*. During crowded holiday periods there's a line, but typically it's less than a five-minute wait to tickle the "ivories" with your toes.

MAKE THE MOST OF YOUR TIME To avoid crowds, shop weekdays
before lunch or during the early afternoon and on weekends, the earlier the better. Also, if there's a wait to enter the Fifth Avenue doors, skip the line by going to Madison and 58th. The doors there are virtually line-free.

767 5th Ave., at 58th St.
Subway: N, R, W to 5th Ave./59th St.

 Free

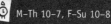 M-Th 10-7, F-Su 10-8

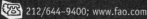 212/644-9400; www.fao.com

 1 and up

From here you can break off into thematic areas that pay tribute to (and have tremendous inventories of) certain toys. The LEGO zone is peppered with larger-than-life brick characters. There are plenty of Barbies in the store, too, with glass displays that show off the doll as she evolved through the ages. Beyond these popular areas there's aisle upon aisle of additional stuffed animals, dolls, and a rather extensive (if underutilized) children's book section.

If you are going to break down and buy something (let's face it, it takes a lot of restraint not to), consider making a Muppet ($99). An experience unique to F.A.O., the Muppet Whatnot Workshop lets kids start with one of several base Muppet bodies, then customize its eyes, nose, hair, and outfit. You can also do this online, but there's obviously a certain satisfaction in having your child design it and have the store build it and hand it over a few minutes later, after the glue dries.

If you like this sight, you may also like Madame Tussauds Wax Museum (#37).

KEEP IN MIND

A section of the store called F.A.O. Schweetz sells assorted candy as well as Pez dispensers and other novelties. But if you're going to indulge your child's sweet tooth you're honestly better off doing it at nearby Dylan's Candy Bar (1011 3rd Ave. at 60th St., tel. 646/735-0078), which has a superior selection.

EATS FOR KIDS
To get a real NYC experience, squeeze into the teeny **Viand Coffee Shop** (2130 Broadway, tel. 212/877-2888). It has the usual diner suspects—grilled cheese, gyros, meat loaf platters—but it's so small you'll wonder how people eat (and live) like this. For an equally good variety but a more spacious dining room, head west to **Mangia** (50 W. 57th St., tel. 212/582-5882) and indulge in antipasto, quesadillas, smoothies, or salads. In warm weather, grab a street table to do some serious people-watching.

I f you want to see one of the only urban islands in the world that's still devoid of commercial entities, condos, and corporations, then you need look no further.

Sitting about a half mile off Manhattan's southern tip, Governor's Island is an oasis of green spaces and biking trails that ranks as one of the city's best kept secrets. Accessible only about 60 days a year, this is one of the prettiest, most pastoral islands that you've never seen.

To reach it, board the free Governor's Island ferry at South Ferry's Battery Maritime Building (the classy little relic situated to the left of the ginormous Staten Island Ferry terminal). The ride over takes about five to seven minutes. Once you arrive, what to do ought to come naturally to any child 10 or under.

The well-tended green spaces invite games of catch (bring a ball or Frisbee), and the grassy hills invite rolling children. Biking on the miles of car-free roads here really is a

EATS FOR KIDS

On-island options usually include a coffee kiosk and beer stand, plus a concession selling burgers and the like (this can be pricey for families and the wait can be long on busy weekends). Consider grabbing deli fare in Lower Manhattan before boarding the ferry.

MAKE THE MOST OF YOUR TIME

The island has a military history. Cannons your kids spy here may have fired some of the first shots in 1776's Battle of Brooklyn, and as you amble around the island you'll catch sight of Castle Williams and Fort Jay, which had roles in wars thereafter. These buildings are really only worth a passing glance, though. Spend most of your time running, biking, or enjoying island programming.

New York Harbor, off southern tip of Manhattan
Subway: 1 to South Ferry; 4,5 to Bowling
Green; R,W to Whitehall St.

 Free

212/440–2200; www.govisland.org

Late May to late Sept., F, Sa, Su; Ferry hourly
F 10–3, last boat back at 5, Sa–Su 10 and 11,
and half-hourly until 5:30, last boat back at 7

 4 and up

must. If you're a local, you are welcome to bring your bike with you on the ferry, but there's also a concession that rents adult and kids bikes on an hourly basis. Tandem and quad bikes are available, too. The latter is recommended if you've got the required four sets of feet in your party; just know that quad biking is a bit harder than it looks, especially if little ones aren't pulling their weight with the pedaling.

While these low-key activities might be enough to keep you busy, there's more. Over the years many organizations have presented art installations and programs, including the Cooper Hewitt National Design Museum and the Children's Museum of the Arts (#54). Most summers there's also free mini-golf and very family-friendly music festivals. But don't worry too much about timing your visit to an event, as it is a pleasure simply being here.

If you like this sight, you may also like the Children's Museum of the Arts (#54).

KEEP IN MIND Governor's Island always seems to be a work in progress. Determined to free up even more space for running and playing, the island is in the process of preparing 30 new acres of park on its southern end that will include baseball fields and a dense, tree-shaded grove with hammocks for kids to good-naturedly fight over.

GREENWAY BIKE/WALKING PATH

J ust as some see the legacy of Robert Moses as highways dividing and destroying communities, some think Bloomberg's legacy will be bicycle lanes and waterfront space reuniting the city's citizens with their green spaces.

The Greenway Path is the best of both initiatives. Part of a car-free biking path that is envisioned to one day stretch 2,500 miles from Maine to Florida, this 13-mile stretch begins near the southern point of Battery Park City and ends past Harlem all the way near Inwood Hill Park. That's pretty much the full length of Manhattan.

While few kids will do the whole path, there are points of interest all along it. Almost anywhere you begin or end will offer something for children. Here are the most interesting, starting from the southernmost tip and ending at the Little Red Lighthouse.

Battery Park City: Someday this path may connect to its cousin on the east side. Until then, start here, where you can bike separate from the frantic NYC traffic. There's enough to

MAKE THE MOST OF YOUR TIME Bikes are available for hourly
and full-day rentals at several places along the path. We suggest **Bike & Roll** (18 Battery Pl., tel. 212/509-0067; www.bikenewyorkcity.com) for the widest selection of family-friendly vehicles. This location operates from 9–7 daily, depending on the season. Verify hours and check alternate rental locations if you aren't beginning your ride downtown.

Entrances include Battery Park City, Pier 84 (42nd), Clinton Cove (55th), and Riverside Park (70th-96th). All are along the Hudson River.
Subway: Battery Park 4, 5 to Bowling Green; 1 to South Ferry

Free; bike rentals range from $8/hour (kid's cycles) to $69/day (tandems, racing bikes)

919/797-0619; www.greenway.org

All ages

keep kids busy for several hours, including the Irish Hunger Memorial, Wintergarden, Nelson Rockefeller Playground, and Tom Otterness sculptures.

Pedal past the West Village and stop at Pier 51's water playground. You may be lucky enough to catch a trapeze class in full swing. Biking past Midtown you can stop at the Dancing Fountain at Pier 84. All along the Upper West Side you'll be in Riverside Park, with several fun sculptures and a great outdoor restaurant, the Boat Basin Cafe. If you make it up to Harlem, the Riverbank State Park has a carousel and two playgrounds. Most people end their ride at "The Little Red Lighthouse and The Great Gray Bridge" (aka Jeffrey's Hook Light and The George Washington Bridge). During warmer months the Urban Rangers will periodically open the lighthouse for visitors.

If you like this sight, you may also like Central Park (#57).

KEEP IN MIND

Like everything in Manhattan, this path is filled with competitive, aggressive people. So even seasoned cyclists might feel like they're on an obstacle course. Teach kids the basics in bike courtesy: how to signal turns or what it means when someone barks out, "On your left!"

EATS FOR KIDS The city developed its waterfronts and its eateries in tandem. In Battery Park City there are several restaurants ranging from fast food to fine dining. Still, we'd suggest you hold out for a picnic alfresco around Pier 54, Chelsea Piers, or Pier 84. If you can wait until then, the **Boat Basin Cafe** (W. 79th St., tel. 212/496-5542) turns out veggie burgers, basic salads, sandwiches, and other kid-faves.

GROUND ZERO AND THE 9/11 MEMORIAL

45

Among the wonderful resources on the Memorial's website are discussion guidelines aimed at parents which include this advice: "It's all right not to know the answer to every question. 9/11 is an incredibly complex subject, with repercussions that are still evolving today. If you can't answer your child's question, be honest."

While it's indeed okay not to have all the answers, it's also okay to preemptively address some questions before arriving. Otherwise your kids may try to fill in the blanks with what they see and hear, whether from volunteers giving tours or a film playing in the visitor center that features 9/11 survivors and their families.

In other words, frame the discussion for your children in your own way before someone else does it for you. That might include avoiding the visitor center altogether, because while it does a good job of showcasing the heroes of 9/11, the uplifting film is quite emotional. Ditto for the 9/11 Museum: Don't go if you're unsure how deeply immersed in the story you want your offspring to be.

EATS FOR KIDS

Eateries around the Ground Zero site are aggressively overpriced, but the **BLT Bar & Grill** (123 Washington St., tel. 646/826–8666) in the W Hotel near the Memorial site, has amazing lunchtime pizzas and the staff is genuinely kind to families.

MAKE THE MOST OF YOUR TIME After visiting the 9/11 Memorial, consider a quick visit to the Trinity Church graveyard (74 Trinity Pl., free), which is a draw for school-aged kids once they learn that Alexander Hamilton is buried there; Robert Fulton is also acknowledged with a memorial. A few blocks south of the church, Fraunces Tavern Museum (54 Pearl St., $7 adults, $4 children 6–17), where George Washington gave his farewell address, has interesting exhibits about colonial America and the Revolutionary War.

Bound by Vesey, Liberty, Church and West Sts.
Subway: E to World Trade Center; R to Rector
St.; A, C, J, Z, 2, 3, 4, 5 to Fulton St.

  Free

 Daily 10–6, last entry at 5; timed-entry
tickets required during construction,
reserve tickets online

212/266-5211;
www.911memorial.org

6 and up

The actual memorial takes up about half of the 16-acre Ground Zero site, and its focal points are the waterfalls and reflecting pools (designated the North Pool and South Pool) set within the footprints of the original twin towers. The names of 9/11 victims and 1993 World Trade Center bombing victims are inscribed around the pools. As you walk around, your kids may naturally run their fingers along the names, dip their hands in the basins of water lining the memorial, or simply stand silently and watch the waterfall. All this behavior is encouraged.

After taking in the reflecting pools, see the nearby Survivor Tree. Found in the wreckage, it was evidently the only tree that survived after the towers fell in 2001—and it survived again after being struck by lightning in 2010, eventually growing taller. Its tale of resilience will likely resonate with your kids well after you leave the site.

If you like this sight, you may also like Ellis Island (#50).

KEEP IN MIND As of this writing, the 9/11 Museum and other parts of Ground Zero were still under construction, meaning that visitors were required to go through airport-style security, have timed-entry tickets (free, printable from the 9/11 Memorial website), and present those tickets at various checkpoints. Prepare your children for these measures if they're still in place. Once construction is completed, the hope is that visitors will be able to come and go to the memorial more freely.

Let's be clear. As achingly conducive as the Guggenheim's six-story spiral ramp would be to running, it is not permitted.

And while kids are good at finding loopholes in this rule by power walking or skipping, that is not encouraged either. This is an oft-crowded space with tourists at every turn. Plus, the interior wall of the spiral is somewhat low even for children who aren't that tall.

Safety tips aside, once you pay your admission, the first order of business should be walking over to the volunteer kiosk in the lobby and borrowing an Activity Pack. These tote bags contain fun puzzles and worksheets that correspond to the art on display. More importantly, there are colored pencils and a sketch pad in there.

Now take the elevator to the sixth floor and work your way down. If your kids are in the mood to sketch, let them. Sitting quietly on the floor in front of the paintings (or in the case of some grown-ups, setting up an easel) is entirely encouraged. But if you see

EATS FOR KIDS **The Wright** restaurant (in the museum, but accessible from a separate entrance if you want to eat first) has a $14 kids meal that's a variation on a sandwich with chips, fruit, and dessert. The restaurant staff is as deferential to children as they are to the grown-ups, which is rare (but quite smart). You can also make a pit stop for a brownie and some coffee at **Cafe 3,** tucked away on the museum's third floor. **Jackson Hole** (1270 Madison Avenue at 91st St., tel. 212/427–2820) is part of a long-time chain in the city somewhat famous for its ample 7-ounce hamburger. It also serves up chicken sandwiches, Mexican dishes, and decent milk shakes.

1071 5th Ave. at 89th St.
Subway: 4, 5, 6 to 86th St.

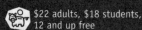 $22 adults, $18 students,
12 and up free

  Su–W and F 10–5:45, Sa 10–7:45

212/423-3500;
www.guggenheim.org

6 and up

a strip of tape on the floor in front of a painting, know that visitors are expected to stay behind it. The artwork is displayed in lots of little alcoves, so kids can sit undisturbed while you stand by and peruse the immediate area.

If the temporary exhibits—on the upper floors—don't pack appeal for your kids, they may change their tune once you get to the second floor's Thannhauser Collection, an ongoing gallery installation with works by Cézanne, Picasso, Renoir, Van Gogh, and Monet, among others. If these do inspire your kids to start sketching (and if they don't probably nothing else in the museum will), it will be fascinating to discover which artists they like the best.

The good news about the sketch pads is that the pages are perforated, which means you can leave with some very special (and free) souvenirs.

If you like this sight, you may also like the Museum of Modern Art (#34).

MAKE THE MOST OF YOUR TIME If you are super-squeezed for time while here or you're detecting a meltdown, begin your visit with the aforementioned (and must-see) Thannhauser Collection on the second floor. If you must prioritize beyond that, also make time for the whimsical Kandinskys on the third floor.

KEEP IN MIND
No photography is permitted above the lobby, and the rule is strictly enforced by guards. That doesn't stop a lot of surreptitious cell phone photography while the guards' backs are turned, but still, best to obey the restrictions.

HIGH LINE

It takes vision and some New York–style persistence to look at an abandoned elevated freight train track and see its potential as a public park. But that's precisely what the Friends of the High Line did when they saved this track from demolition, in part by using a federal loophole that permits former transportation corridors to be used as trails.

Stopping the demolition was only half the battle. After an environmental survey found that no aspect of the track could be used as is, the High Line was completely redesigned and kitted out as an elevated park with benches and chaises, an abundance of plantings and trees, and enough variety and whimsy (a water stream you can run through! funky billboards! a wall of glass!) to delight even young cynics who expect such places to be boring.

As the High Line is a hybrid of a park and a walking trail, you can freely treat it as both. If you're on the West Side and just want to give the park a quick look, you can come and go as you please via stairways at Gansevoort, 14th, 16th, 18th, 20th, 23rd, 26th,

KEEP IN MIND

If you're here in summertime, bees will be loving the foliage as much as you are. You won't encounter an overbearing swarm, but take the same precautions you normally would when traveling with bee-allergic family members and have their bee-sting kits with you.

MAKE THE MOST OF YOUR TIME
At its most crowded (mild summer and spring days or perfect fall ones) the High Line helpfully widens into two lanes to support two-way traffic, if necessary. But don't let dropping temps deter you: In winter (barring closure from foul weather) a snow-topped High Line is a very rare urban pleasure. High Line volunteers have been known to hold snow-sculpting contests—though your family is, of course, free to have your own.

Gansevoort to 30th St.
Subway: A, C, E, L to 14th St./8th Ave.; C, E, to 23rd St.; 1, 2, 3 to 14th St./7th Ave.

 Free

 Daily 7 AM–10 PM

 212/500-6035; www.thehighline.org

4 and up

28th, and 30th Streets (those at 14th, 16th, 23rd, and 30th have elevators). Water fountains are available at various points and there are restrooms at 16th Street.

If you're up for exploring the entire High Line, treat it as a 1.45-mile trail, ascending at Gansevoort Street and descending at 30th Street. Along the way, stop at the scenic overlooks; they offer photo ops and let you take a breather if foot traffic is a little dense. At various points, particularly when you pass under buildings between April and November, you'll find food concessionaires, entertainers, art sellers, and almost always a High Line volunteer who'll happily answer questions about this urban treasure.

If you like this sight, you may also like Carl Schurz Park (#60).

EATS FOR KIDS A grassy patch at the W. 22nd Street section of the trail is perfect for picnicking (if the grass is closed, there are plenty of inviting places near it to sit). Pick up provisions at any of the ubiquitous High Line delis that have mushroomed at the trail's nine access points.

In the heart of Staten Island, this beautiful 100-acre park is another spot that falls into the "well-kept secret" category. The village contains 27 preserved historic buildings and a few reconstructions that interpret three centuries of Staten Island's daily life and culture. Ten buildings are on their original sites (the others were moved from elsewhere on Staten Island), and many of them are open to the public.

The village of Richmond began in the 1690s as a crossroads settlement between scattered farms. The congregation of the Reformed Dutch Church built a combined religious meeting house, school, and residence for its lay minister and teacher around 1695. By 1730 Richmond had become the island's principal political center, and throughout the 18th century the village continued to increase in importance, acquiring a jail, courthouse, churches, taverns, and shops.

KEEP IN MIND If you are traveling in a group with at least 10 kids (grades three through six), you can book your own Mystery Murder and Mischief sleepover here. Families make their own candles, pop their own corn, churn butter, and uncover the back story of one of the most sensational trials in American history. In the very courtroom where Polly Bodine was tried for murder in 1834, they cuddle in their sleeping bags and participate in the dramatic retelling of Polly's mysterious and bizarre trial.

441 Clarke Ave., Staten Island
Subway: 1 to South Ferry, then
S.I. Ferry to SIR train

$5 adults, $3.50 children 5–17 and students

W–Su 1–5; Tours W–F 2:30, Sa–Su 2 and 3:30

718/351–1611;
www.historicrichmondtown.org

All ages

Begin at the 1837 Third County Courthouse Visitor Center to get a guide outlining points of interest. The Historical Museum is in the former County Clerk's Office. The Voorlezer's House is Richmond's oldest building on its original site, as well as the country's oldest elementary schoolhouse. Visitors of all ages marvel at demonstrations of printing, tinsmithing, and other trades performed by artisans in period costumes. Children ages 4 to 10 will enjoy these hands-on activities the most, and may be asked to lend a hand in the Basketmaker's House or help with another chore. When demonstrations aren't happening, a guide is present to give an overview of the setting and answer any questions.

If you like this sight, you may also like National Museum of the American Indian (#31).

EATS FOR KIDS

A picnic area is just east of the visitor center. If you would rather buy food than bring it, try the on-site **Bennett Cafe,** which is open for breakfast on Sunday, lunch on Thursday and Friday, and dinner sporadically. The menu is extremely limited (read: two to four items), but includes standard favorites like grilled cheese or pancakes.

MAKE THE MOST OF YOUR TIME
If you're planning a visit, call to see if any special family events are coming up (reservations are required for some). These include Halloween in Richmond Town, Old Home Day/Harvest Festival, Christmas in Richmond Town, an Independence Day Celebration, Pumpkin Picking at the Decker Farm, and a historic military Encampment Weekend. The Richmond County Fair also takes place here, combining traditional events with modern pastimes.

INTREPID SEA, AIR & SPACE MUSEUM

For many years this aircraft-carrier-cum-museum was a must-do for husbands, sons, and those with a proclivity for the military. But most moms just walked around with that glazed-over look you see when they're dragged to auto shows or comic book conventions.

The *Intrepid* has gone a long way toward rectifying this in recent years by adding narrative elements that make the experience more accessible to the less testosterone-laden members of the public.

Kick off your visit by viewing a short film that shares some of the vessel's long history (built during World War II, it stayed in service until 1974). Next grab an audio tour because listening to the actual pilots and crew members makes the steel and paint come to life. The tour, which leads you around the inside of the vessel, takes between 45 minutes and an hour.

EATS FOR KIDS

If you're biking the Greenway (#46), there are several good refueling spots en route. If not, try the **Sullivan Street Bakery** (533 W. 47th St., tel. 212/929–5900) about three blocks away. Its flatbread pizzas make a fine lunch-on-the-go, just save room for the *bombolinis*—Italian-style doughnuts.

KEEP IN MIND Check to make sure there are no major patriotic events taking place during your visit. The *Intrepid* is frequently closed or crowded for ones like Veterans Day or Fleet Week. News-making figures (Prince Harry, Hillary Clinton, and Buzz Aldrin among them) sometimes appear at such events. So when you're onboard, you'll be retracing famous footsteps. If you're more impressed by movie stars, you'll be pleased to know that Nicolas Cage also shot a memorable sequence for *National Treasure* here. The *Intrepid* also appeared in Will Smith's *I Am Legend*.

Pier 86, 12th Ave. and 46th St.
Subway: 1, 2, 3 to 42nd St./Times Square;
A, C, E to 42nd St./8th Ave.

  $24 adults, $20 students,
$17 children 7–17 and
veterans, $12 kids 3–6; free
children under 3, U.S. active
military, retired U.S. military

Apr–Oct, M–F 10–5, Sa–Su 10–6;
Nov–Mar, daily 10–5; closed M

212/245-0072;
www.intrepidmuseum.org

 5 and up

A thrill for most visitors is, naturally, the planes on the deck. As it can get crowded, allow plenty of time to inspect the 30 vintage aircraft. Highlights include a walk through the Concorde (who knew it was so small inside?) and seeing the world's fastest plane (the A-12 Blackbird spy plane, which flies at 2,269 miles per hour).

The planes likely would have remained the biggest draw here had it not been for the museum's acquisition in 2012 of the space shuttle *Enterprise*. In retirement, she sits on the carrier's flight deck enrobed by a pavilion. The shuttle is suspended far enough off the ground for visitors to take a peek underneath, and there is also a viewing platform in case your curious kids want to get a bit closer. Regrettably for the children (and the child in all of us), climbing aboard the shuttle is not yet permitted.

If you like this sight, you may also like the New York Transit Museum (#21).

MAKE THE MOST OF YOUR TIME The *Intrepid* once accommodated up to 3,388 crew members and so was basically the equivalent of a small town—a concept that your kids will better appreciate if you do a little prep work before coming. Excellent teacher resources on the ship's website includes a "Life at Sea" primer that's full of fun tidbits. When you're ready to visit, arrive as early as you can because tours fill up quickly. Note that this is an ideal stop during a Greenway bike trip (#46), as there are plenty of bike racks and a big splash fountain for kids to play in.

The curators make this a kid-friendly place by taking objects and people representative of "the Jewish experience" and spinning them into a universal story, applicable to everyone regardless of religion, race, or nationality.

Take the recent Curious George Saves the Day exhibit. Aside from displaying many original illustrations from the beloved books, it also revealed how its Jewish authors (Margaret and H.A. Rey) escaped the Nazis thanks to the Curious George illustrations in their suitcases. The Houdini: Art and Magic exhibit, similarly, demonstrated how this Hungarian Jew (the son of a rabbi) morphed from a fledgling circus performer into the world's most famous magician. Although his secrets weren't revealed, many of his magic apparatus were on display. Simply put, there is always at least one exhibit so evocative that children will momentarily forget they're in a museum.

The permanent exhibit, Culture and Continuity: The Jewish Journey, has 800 objects showcasing international Jewish identity. While younger kids may not stay focused through

MAKE THE MOST OF YOUR TIME Plan to spend at least 45 minutes at Archaeology Zone: Discovering Treasures from Playgrounds to Palaces. Here kids live the life of an archaeologist by interpreting symbols in a colorful mosaic, creating works of art inspired by objects in the museum's collection, or dressing in costumes. The exhibit includes an introductory video as well as original artifacts, and the emphasis on archaeological methods makes it appealing to young Indiana Jones wannabes.

1109 5th Ave., at 92nd St.
Subway: 4, 5, 6 to 86th St

 212/423-3200; www.
thejewishmuseum.org

 $12 adults, $7.50 students
13 and up, free Sa

 F-T 11-5:45, Th 11-8
(Archaeology Zone closed Sa)

 2 and up

the whole trip, its worth a quick visit. Little visitors tend to find the re-creation of an ancient synagogue of interest, whereas older children enjoy television and radio programs from the museum's broadcast archive, as well as a film on Jewish rituals that's screened in a gallery filled with ceremonial objects.

During the week there are several art and culture workshops available for children of different ages. Most include a walk around the current kid-friendly exhibit and then a studio session to make art. There are also occasional family art programs, geared toward kids three to seven, that include a children's book reading and art activity.

Note that this museum is one of the few open on Monday (it closes Saturday instead).

If you like this sight, you may also like the Lower East Side Tenement Museum (#38).

KEEP IN MIND

Around special events, both Jewish and non-Jewish holidays, there are family celebrations and themed happenings. For example, at Hanukkah kids can make their own glowing menorah using low-tech electronics.

EATS FOR KIDS Lunch, snacks, and a light dinner are available at the museum's *glatt* (that means ultimate) kosher **Cafe Weissman**. For something more novel, try the **Barking Dog Luncheonette** (1678 3rd Ave., tel. 212/831-1800), offering breakfast, lunch, dinner, and brunch. The puppy-themed decor entrances young ones, and a drinking fountain just for canines provides a constant dog parade. Try a burger on focaccia bread, meat loaf, or a yogurt sundae with granola topping.

LIBERTY SCIENCE CENTER

Science and Sociology Center is more like it. Kids, and most adults, will love the fact that this facility focuses on application, not theory.

There are two animal exhibitions: Our Hudson Home and Eat and Be Eaten, where children can see live animals and learn more about the adaptations critters employ to capture prey and avoid being gobbled up themselves. As they say here, poison, camouflage, hide and seek, and other weapons of warfare have been used in the natural world for far longer than human beings have been using them in the military one.

Favorite science museum activities, like making enormous soap bubbles and balancing a ball on a blowing stream of air, are part of the Wonder Why exhibit. Considering it has a rock-climbing wall as an added perk, you shouldn't have any trouble keeping kids under 10 busy for a while.

EATS FOR KIDS

Enjoy great views and light meals at the on-site **Café Skylines**. The menu lists soup, sandwiches, and standard kiddie fare (think chicken fingers or hot dogs). If you've brought a bag lunch, ask at the welcome desk about indoor or outdoor spots to unpack your picnic.

KEEP IN MIND This is a perfect complement to the New York Hall of Science, with its emphasis on deconstructing science from a kid's perspective. The center's main question is "How does this work?," focusing on the human interplay with science, answering "How do we impact science and how does science impact us?"

Liberty State Park, 222 Jersey City Blvd., Jersey City, NJ
Subway: PATH train to Pavonia/Newport or Exchange
Place, then Hudson-Bergen Light Rail to Liberty
State Park

 $16.75 adults, $12.50
children 2-12; IMAX
and 3-D show extra

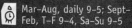 Mar-Aug, daily 9-5; Sept-
Feb, T-F 9-4, Sa-Su 9-5

 2 and up

201/200-1000; www.lsc.org

Kids who are older (or especially brave) can make tracks for the pitch-black Touch Tunnel. An interactive experience that can best be described as a sensory-deprivation maze, it is 80 feet of tubing that children crawl through using only their sense of touch. In a true nod to what moves contemporary kids, maze survivors have the option of posting to social media infrared images of themselves in the tunnel.

And that's just the first act. With an IMAX theater (not suitable for kids under 6), live science demonstrations (featuring audience volunteers), more than a dozen exhibitions, and a slew of special events (including sleepovers in winter), this place is well worth a PATH train ticket, especially on bad-weather days.

Need an added incentive? You can climb up to the top-floor Observation Deck to snap a photo with clear views of Ellis Island, Manhattan, and the Statue of Liberty as a backdrop.

If you like this sight, you may also like the New York Hall of Science (#24).

MAKE THE MOST OF YOUR TIME Kids 6 to 15
will get the most out of a visit. Print out the age-appropriate official "Liberty
Science Center Scavenger Hunt" from the website. Upon completion, par-
ticipants earn the title of "Scientist for a Day" and get a certificate recognizing
their efforts. Visitors with younger children can also find an online section with
tips targeted specifically at the under-five set.

LOWER EAST SIDE TENEMENT MUSEUM

38

Although the goal here is giving kids an appreciation for immigrant life in America, the bonus is something much more practical, if less noble: serious ammo the next time they whine about sharing space with siblings.

Chronicling a variety of immigrant experiences in Manhattan's Lower East Side, this urban living-history museum is only accessible by joining one of six tours, each representing a different family's experience.

For example, the Confino family tour (for ages five and older) uses a costumed interpreter to share the joys and hardships of tenement life. Picture 10 people living in three rooms, all totaling less than the square footage of the average suburban garage; washing their hair on the fire escape; chasing rats out with a broom; and sharing a toilet with almost everyone in the building.

But the tour chronicles good times, too. Hence your kids can play a real Victrola in the Confino's apartment and listen in as the Confino's daughter vividly describes what she does

EATS FOR KIDS The Lower East Side is a wonderland of kid-friendly delights specializing in the actual food immigrants ate back in the day. Get knishes (dough pockets like calzones) or potato latkes (pancakes) at **Yonah Schimmel's Knishery** (137 E. Houston St., tel. 212/477–2858), a Lower East Side institution that began from a pushcart. For dim sum or veggie dumplings, try the **Dumpling House** (118A Eldridge St., tel. 212/625–8008). Top it all off by getting a sugar rush at **Economy Candy** (108 Rivington St., tel. 212/254–1531), a store packed floor to ceiling with favorite old-time candies, international treats, and bulk sweets.

Visitor Center, 103 Orchard St., entrance on Delancey St.; tenement, 97 Orchard St.

Subway: B, D to Grand St.; F to Delancey St.; J, M, X to Essex St.

212/982–8420; www.tenement.org

Tour $22 adults, $17 students

Tours 10–5

8 and up

in the few moments of free time she has—including going to Coney Island or the local nickelodeon to watch silent films.

The other tenement tours tell the story of immigrants from Germany, Ireland, and Italy. Families can also take a Next Steps neighborhood walking tour to learn more about the Lower East Side from 1935 to the present. Such options, however, are suggested for ages eight and up or 12 and up (depending on the tour) as there are no live actors to engage the children.

The commercial side of the immigrant experience also got some attention when Shop Life opened in spring 2012. The exhibit examines three of the 30 immigrant-owned businesses that came and went over a 100-year period at 97 Orchard Street. One highlight is a recreated 1870s beer saloon. The exhibit also includes a long counter with interactive touch-screens that lets kids uncover the history behind various objects once found in these shops.

If you like this sight, you may also like Ellis Island (#50).

KEEP IN MIND

Tour tickets (available on a first-come, first-served basis) sell out quickly, as groups are limited to 15. Tickets for weekday tours and programs may be purchased in advance online or by phone (tel. 866/811–4111). Call the visitor center for details about multi-tour discounts on advance tickets.

MAKE THE MOST OF YOUR TIME Make this your one

day to do the Lower East Side. It's an ideal New York City neighborhood to explore from a historical perspective because it offers a classic mix of old-school immigrant shops and super hipster boutiques. Visit **Russ & Daughters** (179 E. Houston St., tel. 212/475–4880), in business since 1914 and still serving killer babka, or **The Pickle Guys** (49 Essex St., tel. 212/656–9739) with 15+ varieties of pickles picked from barrels.

MADAME TUSSAUDS WAX MUSEUM

Will and Kate, The Duke and Duchess of Cambridge, await your arrival here, as does actor Daniel Craig, all looking as dashing and lifelike as ever.

And next to Mr. Craig, is that *Saturday Night Live* funnyman Seth Meyers? Well actually, no, it's sometimes funnyman Hugh Grant (it sure looked like Seth Meyers) which goes to show that not every wax recreation here hits the mark. But most come close enough.

The likenesses are pretty darn good at the Opening Night Party, for instance, where your brood can impress Facebook friends by uploading pics of your wild night in New York City with Angelina Jolie and Brad Pitt.

Young moviegoers may prefer the Pirates of the Caribbean: Dead Man's Chest room, meant to replicate the famous *Black Pearl* ship from the Johnny Depp flick. Or, perhaps, Superman Returns will be more their style. It's housed in a giant dome theater intricately decorated like Metropolis. Children enter through a phone booth, and can pretend they're Superman as a subway car levitates in midair, inviting them to stand under and "lift" it.

MAKE THE MOST OF YOUR TIME

This is more like an exhibit than a whole museum. You follow a linear path through the displays, and backtracking, while possible, is not a graceful experience. Take photos, and take your time, with the "people" you encounter. You may never meet them again.

KEEP IN MIND Marie Tussaud (the titular Madame) got her start making death masks of guillotined nobles during the French Revolution. Today the model-making process is considerably less painful for subjects—but it's still painstaking for those who sculpt the museum's wax figures. It takes four months to create one, including 140 hours for artists to carefully insert individual strands of hair. Many celebrities donate clothes for their own figures. Joan Rivers even donated her favorite nail polish to make a perfect match. Once on exhibit, each wax portrait is inspected and groomed daily, and its hair is washed and makeup retouched regularly.

234 W. 42nd St.
Subway: 1, 2, 3, 7, N, Q, R, W, S
to 42nd St./Times Square

 $30 ages 13 and up,
$23 children 4–12

Su–Th 10–8, F–Sa 10–10

 5 and up

212/512-9600; www.nycwax.com

Rather hobnob with the world's intellectual and political elite? Luminaries in the Gallery include Ghandi, the Dalai Lama, Nelson Mandela, and the Pope. Take a picture in the Oval Office with President Obama and the First Lady (if you're nice to the museum guard, he'll snap a group photo of you and your kids with them).

Children curious about how these figures were created can also check out the Behind the Scenes exhibit, where they'll learn what it takes to make an ultra-realistic wax model from measurement to makeup.

The SCREAM attraction, filled with actors impersonating characters from popular horror films, is probably an experience best reserved for mature teens. The less threatening Marvel 4-D zone involves kids in an interactive experience with their favorite Marvel character (they can, for instance, wield Thor's hammer). But honestly, both of these are skippable, especially since you have to pay extra for them, above the cost of the already pricey general admission.

If you like this sight, you may also like the Sony Wonder Technology Lab (#10).

EATS FOR KIDS Times Square is lined with chain restaurants. If you're content with Appleby's, Red Lobster, or Chevy's, all are within an easy one block. For a more local experience, grab falafel at **Maoz** (558 7th Ave., tel. 212/777–0820) and find a table in the Broadway Pedestrian Precinct.

METROPOLITAN MUSEUM OF ART

Claudia Kincaid, an 11-year-old New Yorker, feeling unappreciated, decides to run away from home. The discomforts of runaway life, however, aren't her style. So she decides to make the "Met" her new home.

Even kids who haven't read *The Mixed Up Files of Mrs. Basil E. Frankweiler* (required reading before a visit) can relate. This may be the Western Hemisphere's biggest museum, but if your kids are initiated the right way, they'll want to move right in, too.

Don't devote too much time to the painting galleries. Sure, there are plenty of old masters, new masters, plus paintings you didn't even know were masters, and you'll want to at least say you did it. But from a kid's point of view, the real treasures can't be hung on a wall. Instead, focus your time on these highlights before kids get museumed-out.

Egyptian Art: This may well be the best part of the visit as it promises a chance to go into a real Egyptian temple (the Temple of Dendur), plenty of mummies, coffins, cats, hieroglyphics, sphinxes, and William the Hippopotamus.

EATS FOR KIDS Staying in the museum for lunch makes it easier to resume your artsy afternoon. **The American Wing Café** is the best mix of casual atmosphere and refined food, and it offers a nice view. The self-serve **cafeteria** is for kids who will only eat chicken fingers or fries. If you're ready to call it quits, head out to experience an old-fashioned soda jerk—one of the very few left in NYC—the **Lexington Candy Shop** (1226 Lexington Ave., tel. 212/288–0057). The milk shakes and malts are fun, even if the burgers and fries are unremarkable.

5th Ave. and 82nd St.
Subway: 4, 5, 6 to 86th St.

 Suggested donation $25 adults,
$12 students 12 and up

 T-Th and Su 9:30–5:30, F-Sa 9:30–9

212/535-7710; www.
metmuseum.org

 4 and up

Equestrian Court & Hall of Arms: Let imaginations run wild as kids explore the castle-like courtyard with its knights riding brave steeds, both completely covered in shining armor.

American Wing: A giant atrium filled with fountains, sculptures, gaslights, and the entire facade of the Branch Bank of the United States that once stood at 15½ Wall Street. Off to the side are period rooms showing kids how families (well, at least wealthy ones) lived over the past few centuries.

In summer the roof garden usually has something of interest to children, whether it's a 60-foot bamboo building kids can tour or Jeff Koons' gigantic Balloon Dog. Of course, the entire family can appreciate the sweeping view.

If you like this sight, you may also like the Museum of Modern Art (#34).

MAKE THE MOST OF YOUR TIME

If you had three weeks to do nothing but this museum, you'd still find more to do. Try to decide in advance which galleries are going to interest your family most (the website includes handy floor plans and suggested family itineraries); then allocate time accordingly.

KEEP IN MIND Preparing in advance for your visit will make it more memorable. Visit the "Museum Kids" section on the Met's website. There you'll find family podcasts meant for four- to nine-year-olds presenting small stories about one item or collection. Download several Family Guides and use them to plot out what you'll see and when. The Explore & Learn activities are multimedia storybooks. Finally, the website lists in detail all family activities and programs available during your visit. Wait until you arrive to get the hard copy of the Family Map, it has a terrific "I Spy" game on the back.

MOTT STREET

ott Street is Chinatown's unofficial main drag, where Chinese immigrants first settled in tenements in the 1880s, leaving their descendants a street achingly dense with storefronts and evocative city blocks.

Mott is where you'll end up for prime snacking and souvenir shopping, but the walk here is part of the fun. Exit the Canal Street subway station at the corner of Canal and Lafayette Streets. Look toward Centre Street and up to your left at the red pagoda-like building with three jagged roofs on top and a Starbucks below. Welcome to Chinatown old and new.

Continue on Canal through the Centre intersection, passing some underwhelming shops on your left until reaching Baxter. Off to the right, where Canal, Baxter, and Walker Streets meet, is another pagoda-like structure: handily, an information kiosk. As you walk toward the kiosk, the **Dragon Land Bakery** (125 Walker St. between Centre and Baxter Sts.) beckons from diagonally across the street with pastries ranging from the sweet to the what-is-that-meat?-filled variety. Grab a few at random and emerge onto Walker,

EATS FOR KIDS

If you're drawn by the promise of quality dim sum, head to **Ping Seafood** (22 Mott St., just past Mosco St., tel. 212/602–9988) for hot, juicy dumplings dabbed in salty soy sauce. Non–dim sum lovers can order off the menu.

MAKE THE MOST OF YOUR TIME The walk from the Canal Street station to this tour's endpoint on Mosco Street is only about a half mile as the crow flies. The amount of time it takes to walk there (and back, if you're returning to Canal) will obviously depend on how long you linger. Leave at least three hours so that you can snack, shop, have lunch, shop, and snack some more before continuing on to your next stop.

Mott St., bound by Canal and Mosco Sts.
Subway: 6, J,Z, N, Q, R to Canal St.

 212/346-9288; www.
explorechinatown.com

 Free

 Daily, weekday mornings are best

 5 and up

heading toward Mulberry. Canal will run parallel on your left, with Walker petering out until you're back on Canal. Keep walking.

At this point your family's sense of smell will go into overdrive as you pass fish markets that often have runaway crabs skittering across the sidewalk. Continue on Canal after passing Mulberry, walking by various shops until reaching the intersection of Canal and Mott. Make a right, at which point you'll be walking south.

Continue on Mott, grazing souvenir shops full of paw-waving kitties, faux jade figurines, wallets, and toys inexpensive enough to buy at will. Continue south on Mott, passing Bayard and Pell, until you reach Mosco. From here, you can continue south if you're visiting the 9/11 Memorial (#45) and its environs. Otherwise, turn around and work the other side of Mott Street.

If you like this sight, you may also like the Lower East Side Tenement Museum (#38).

KEEP IN MIND If you're heading back toward your starting point at the Canal Street station, consider making a detour to Pearl Paint (308 Canal St., tel. 212/431–7932), a walk-up with floor upon floor of art supplies, serving both serious painters and amateur dabblers. If your kids are easily seduced by trips to office supply stores, they will especially like the deep selection of pens, sketchpads, drawing kits, and other painterly accoutrements that you'd be hard pressed to find elsewhere in the city.

MUSEUM OF MODERN ART

This place divides into two camps: "Yay!" or "Yawn."

Whether the Museum of Modern Art, aka the MoMA, is sheer delight or pure torture for kids depends on your planning skills, current exhibits, and when you go. The MoMA tries to pull kids into modern art from the cradle. Recent initiatives have reinforced their mission: They've introduced kids' audio tours, expanded family programming, added an indoor drop-in Shape Lab, and made several downloadable gallery guides for their website.

Begin with the most kid-friendly exhibits. In recent years MoMA has pushed its populism by doing at least one temporary installation with wide appeal. Galleries displaying Tim Burton's madcap creations (think fluorescent spinning tops, cartoons, and costumes from his movies) were a big hit with kids, as was a Century of the Child exhibit that examined the design history of toys and games.

Sculpture, especially the modern variety with its tactile tentacles, oversize body parts, and strange placement—a bicycle wheel growing out of a stool?—is also appealing. Since

EATS FOR KIDS Cafe 2 is such a good value for kids. For $6, children get handmade pasta in butter or a fresh marinara sauce, and it's big enough for siblings to share. Adult meals are slightly more (around $11) but with options like artisanal cheese plates, wild-mushroom tart, and pan-seared salmon, it's still a good deal. Plentiful seating and fast service make this an even better bet.

11 W. 53rd St., between, 5th and 6th Aves.
Subway: B, D, F to 47–50th Sts./Rockefeller
Center; E, M to 53rd St./5th Ave.

212/708-9400; www.moma.org

 $25 ages 17 and up,
$14 students 17 and up;
free F 4–8

W–Th and Sa–M 10:30–5:30,
F 10:30–8

 4 and up

many of the more kid-accessible sculptures shares gallery space with the paintings, adults can glimpse famous modernists like Klee, Matisse, and Picasso while kids gaze at a real helicopter overhead. (Yes, this is another sculpture.)

If you can handle the crowds, go on a weekend to experience the extensive family programming. Every Saturday and Sunday there are drop-in Tours for Fours and A Closer Look for Kids workshops. Tour leaders follow a theme as they take families to four or five works in the gallery. At each piece there is a discussion paired with a small art project. In the theater at noon they screen short family-friendly films you won't see elsewhere—all have artistic themes and there is usually a discussion in between. Such programs are free with admission. For children seven and under, the ground-level Shape Lab allows kids to play with shapes in different media (computers, magnetic Colorforms, furniture, blocks).

If you like this sight, you may also like the Guggenheim (#44).

KEEP IN MIND
MoMA's gift shops are two of the best in the city, well worth the splurge. Here you'll find everyday objects with an aesthetic twist, funky kids toys, and a fun selection of artistic picture books.

MAKE THE MOST OF YOUR TIME
Before you go, check out the excellent "Planning Your Visit with a Family" section of the museum's website. It's fairly comprehensive, and includes helpful recommendations, like how long to visit with a child (30–90 minutes) or the least crowded times to go (morning, weekdays).

33

Kids like this museum because it chronicles their everyday life, and its collections are filled with tangible items they can relate to.

Both this and its cousin on Central Park West (the New-York Historical Society, #23) exist primarily to codify New York City. But, whereas the historical society approaches its subject from the perspective of personality and politics, this museum focuses on daily life.

A good way to begin your visit—and bone up on NYC's backstory—is by watching the all-ages-appropriate, 22-minute film *Timescapes: A Multi-Media Portrait of New York*, which runs every half-hour from 10:15 to 4:15. Projected on three screens in a specially designed theater, it documents more than four centuries of the city's development from its origins as a tiny settlement of Native Americans to today's megalopolis.

KEEP IN MIND

At PROTECT! kids learn how fire and fire safety have shaped the Big Apple over four centuries by seeing bucket brigades, hose carriages, and pumpers that were pulled not by horses but by firefighters.

EATS FOR KIDS

One perk of the NYC melting pot culture is the glorious range of cuisine. Try something new at **Lechonera El Barrio** (172 E. 103rd St., tel. 212/722–1344). Adults can experiment with Puerto Rican specialties such as *relleno de papa*, *mofongo de pollo*, and *batido de mamey*. Less adventurous kids can always fall back on rice and beans.

1220 5th Ave., at 103rd St.
Subway: 6 to 103rd St.; 2, 3 to 110th St.

 Suggested donation $20 families,
$10 adults, $6 students 13 and up

 10–6

212/534–1672; www.mcny.org

 4 and up

Plenty of the museum's 1.5 million+ items spanning 400 years of NYC history appeal to kids. Show them seats from the original Yankee Stadium, a 1980 Checker cab, a piece of the old mechanical Times Square news "zipper," or a giant bolt tightener used to build the Brooklyn Bridge.

Given that this is such a famously "in your face" town, it might be worthwhile to linger in the exhibit Activist New York, which through photos, video, and artifacts gives an approachable look at social activism in all five boroughs of the city from the 17th century to the present.

On the first and third Sunday of every month there is usually a family program thematically connected to an exhibit. Recent ones have included historical looks at printmaking (with opportunities for children to craft prints of their own) and a history of the East River.

If you like this sight, you may also like the New-York Historical Society (#23).

MAKE THE MOST OF YOUR TIME Although it
is at the opposite end of the city, you will get an even more robust look at the museum's collection if you head down to the South Street Seaport Museum (#9), whose galleries are operating under the auspices of the Museum of the City of New York.

A projector stands at the ready, waiting for your children to make a five-second video that can be turned into a flip book. Across from this is an 1899 mutoscope—a contraption with still photos attached to a wheel whose crank, when turned, yields a flip-book style movie. In a room off to the side, computers enable kids to make LEGO stop-motion animation movies, or "hack" Web pages.

That's when it hits you. This museum isn't just a tribute to movies as motion pictures: It's a salute to every kind of moving image, past and present. Moreover, it offers ocular proof that a single image—in some cases screenshots or crayon drawings your child makes here—can be set in motion to create something magical.

The core permanent exhibit, Behind the Screen, explores how motion pictures and TV programs are created. But even kids who couldn't care less about the process may squeal with delight at seeing an actual head from a *Star Wars* Chewbacca costume or a real Yoda puppet. Likewise, parents may squeal with nostalgia over the display of face masks Robin Williams wore in *Mrs. Doubtfire* or the costume he wore in *Mork and Mindy*.

KEEP IN MIND In the ADR (automated dialog replacement) Studio, children can replace bits of dialogue in scenes from different movies with their own voices, always with hilarious results. Once kids realize how cool this is, the wait (even among your own children) can be frustrating as the process takes a few minutes and some kids may be tempted have another go. Try the activity once, give someone else a turn, and do it again on the way out. Note that younger kids will need help from a parent or older sibling.

36-01 35th Avenue, at 37th St., Astoria, Queens
Subway: M (weekdays only), R to Steinway St.;
Q (weekdays only), N to 36th Ave.

$12 adults, $9 students, $6 children 3–12; free F 4–8

T-Th 10-5, F 10:30-8, Sa-Su 11:30-7

718/777-6888; www.movingimage.us

6 and up

Interactive workstations within the exhibit let kids experiment with various audio and video techniques. (Mercifully, operating them doesn't require help from a manual or a museum employee—parents can actually assist if necessary.) With the aforementioned LEGO stop-motion animation, a child as young as six can figure out the software.

Kids will also want to linger at wall of classic arcade games like Pong, Space Invaders, and Super Breakout, which—parents will appreciate—are arranged chronologically, flashing them back to moments in their lives the way certain songs do. Several of the games are free to play, while others require tokens that you can buy from a machine. Aside from tokens and the cost of a flip book (available for purchase in the gift shop), you won't encounter any add-on fees here.

If you like this sight, you may also like the Sony Wonder Technology Lab (#10).

MAKE THE MOST OF YOUR TIME
The museum screens 20-minute movie serials, such as black-and-white Dick Tracy capers, in the neo-Egyptian Cleopatra's Theater. Although kids enjoy these more than you'd expect, waiting around for the movie to start and the actual movie experience is not essential to your visit, unless you honestly need a spot to rest for 20 minutes or so.

EATS FOR KIDS
In addition to the juicy burgers for which it was named, **Five Napkin Burger** (35-01 36th St., tel. 718/433-2727) serves sushi, salads, and a decent weekend brunch. For a taste of Astoria history (and tender lamb), try **Uncle George's Greek Tavern** (33-19 Broadway, tel. 718/626-0593), a lively 24/7 diner.

NATIONAL MUSEUM OF THE AMERICAN INDIAN

Buying Manhattan for $24?

This Dutch "bargain" was no more legit than purchasing an iPad that "fell off the truck." Native Americans, lacking the same land ownership beliefs as European explorers, were really just offering to share use of the land.

Beyond appealing to children's natural curiosity about other cultures, the local branch of the Washington D.C. Smithsonian Institution clears up this and other popular misconceptions about Native Americans, largely through personal interaction.

As part of the Institution's mission to empower the Indian voice, this place hosts more live family-friendly programs than almost any NYC museum, and that's the main reason to come.

Throughout the year kids can meet Native Americans across nations and tribes through dances, hands-on workshops, concerts, and storytelling programs. These participation-

KEEP IN MIND

Popular annual events include a Children's Festival, a Summer Dance program (two dance performances daily throughout July), the concert series Native Sounds Downtown, and, around Halloween, an annual two-day celebration of the Latin American festival Day of the Dead.

EATS FOR KIDS Pick up salad-bar food (sandwiches, salads, or soups) at **Zaytuna** (17 Battery Pl., tel. 212/871–6300), a few blocks from the museum. Take it to Battery Park across the street, and enjoy a picnic overlooking the water. A few blocks away, Stone Street (considered to be this area's restaurant row) has several sit-down options. Try **Adrienne's Pizza Bar** (54 Stone St., tel. 212/248–3838) to sample their delicious rectangular pizza.

George Gustav Heye Center, 1 Bowling Green
Subway: 4, 5 to Bowling Green; 1 to South Ferry;
2, 3 to Wall St.; R to Whitehall St.; J, Z to Broad St.

 Free

 10–5 daily, Th until 8, closed Dec. 25

212/514-3700; www.americanindian.si.edu

5 and up

heavy events encourage children to ask questions and learn about native beliefs, history, legends, and lifestyles.

Visitors with younger children start at the Resource Center, a family-oriented room filled with materials that help make the visit more fun and give it context at the same time. Kids love to play with the computers loaded with interactive exhibits (these can be accessed at home as well), do the art projects, and read picture books. Often there are cultural interpreters on hand.

Children also enjoy browsing the museum's only permanent exhibit, Infinity of Nations, because the majority of objects were made for everyday use, of familiar materials, and have an animal theme. Allow 30 to 45 minutes to walk around the two floors looking at carved animal figures, elaborate clothes, feathers, baskets, and painted hides. Adults should be sure to look up at the frescoes painted on the rotunda wall. The neoclassical building itself is impressive and the interior even more so.

If you like this sight, you may also like the American Museum of Natural History (#68).

MAKE THE MOST OF YOUR TIME
As there are really only two places to take kids (the permanent exhibit and the Resource Center), this museum can easily be done in an hour or less. Consider passing through on your way to the Statue of Liberty or other points of interest downtown. It's free, so there's nothing to lose if you breeze through quickly.

NBC STUDIOS TOUR

Television fans must take this tour. Although you probably won't see any stars, you will get a behind-the-scenes glimpse at one of American's most powerful networks.

Tours start by rewinding time and taking you back to NBC's birth in the Golden Age of Radio. Then you'll visit the saccharine '40s and '50s shows your parents may have grown up on. At last, you'll enter one to three studios where they currently film popular shows like *Saturday Night Live*, *Late Night with Jimmy Fallon*, *NBC Nightly News*, the *Today Show*, and the pregame show *Football Night in America*. You can also learn about the latest TV technology used to broadcast around the world.

Purchase tickets in advance to guarantee your preferred day and time. Many groups book ahead, so if you do choose to purchase your tickets on the day of your tour, you'll need to get here early. Tours are often sold out by early afternoon.

EATS FOR KIDS At the **Rock Center Café** (20 W. 50th St., tel. 212/332–7620), ask for a seat overlooking the skating rink in winter, the garden in spring or summer. While it's part of a mini-chain, **Potbelly Sandwich Shop** (30 Rockefeller Plaza, tel. 646/289–4203) turns out respectable hot and toasty sandwiches. **Prime Burger** (5 E. 51st St., tel. 212/759–4729) serves filling burgers, shakes, and pies.

30 Rockefeller Plaza, 49th St. between 5th and 6th Aves.
Subway: B, D, F, M to 47th–50th Sts./Rockefeller Center

 M–Th 8:30–5:30, F–Sa 8:30–6:30, Su 9:15–4:30, tours depart every 15 minutes

 212/664-3700, 212/664-3056 NBC tickets; www.nbcstudiotour.com

 $24 adults, $21 children 6–12

6 and up

NBC has been offering these tours since 1933. And even if you don't rub shoulders with a present-day NBC celebrity, you might be led around by a future one! An NBC page serves as your guide, and former pages have included Ted Koppel, Willard Scott, Regis Philbin, Steve Allen, Kate Jackson, and Michael Eisner.

If you like this sight, you may also like the behind-the-scenes tour at Radio City Music Hall (#15).

KEEP IN MIND

Check www.nbcstudiotour.com before you come to see if any celebrity signings, new product unveilings, or other special events are slated to be held on the day of your tour.

MAKE THE MOST OF YOUR TIME

Schedule a whole "Rockefeller Center Day." Since this area of the city has a high concentration of kid-friendly attractions, you can combine the tour with a visit to Radio City Music Hall (#15), Top of the Rock and the Rockefeller Center Ice Rink (#13), or the windows of Saks Fifth Avenue (during holiday time). Start early, so you'll have plenty of energy.

NEW VICTORY THEATER

Once the house lights dim there's no way you'll confuse this theater with the Disney one across the street. Any umbrella-toting nannies or undersea princesses appearing on stage are either going to be shadow puppets or Shakespearean sprites.

The New Victory staff travels the globe, literally, to find thought-provoking, edgy productions transcending traditional tropes, roles, and plots. The theater itself had a racy past: It was Broadway's first burlesque house in 1933, and then, in the '70s, Times Square's first XXX theater. But all that's history, and these days it's New York's preeminent venue for intelligent, sophisticated performances aimed at the under-18 crowd. Adults often enjoy them as much as the kids do. The ultra-reasonable prices make them happy, too. Rarely is a ticket above $35—a real steal compared to Broadway musicals—and if it's part of a subscription it can come close to half that.

Recent productions have included the preschool-geared puppet show *Grug* (ages two to five); *Mojo*, where objects musically spring to life and discover, yes, their mojo

KEEP IN MIND
The family workshops accompanying most shows sell out almost immediately. Try to get on the email list to be notified when registration is open.

MAKE THE MOST OF YOUR TIME
Visiting the website before booking is a must-do. Every single performance page has a directory of features to help you decide if a show is right for your kids: a video, short summary, and show dates plus info on length, narrative type, age recommendations and more.

209 W. 42nd St., west of Broadway
Subway: 1, 2, 3, 7, N, Q, R, W, S to
42nd St./Times Square

Regular ticket prices $14–$38,
member ticket prices $9–$25,
varying by performance

Times vary

646/223-3020; www.newvictory.org

All ages, but varies
by production

(five and up); *Puss in Boots,* an operatic puppet show (eight and up); *Nevermore,* a surrealistic recounting of events shaping Edgar Allan Poe's life (11 and up); the Shakespearean comedy *As You Like It* (12 and up); *Squirm Burpee Circus,* a vaudeville pandemonium (all ages); and *Zoo Zoo,* featuring dancers so skilled that you'd forget they aren't the animals they're portraying.

Performances usually have corresponding workshops ($17), where children become acquainted with what they are going to see by practicing a few of the skills the performers themselves will demonstrate on stage. For example, learning hip-hop moves or bringing puppets to life. Workshops sell out quickly, so reserve them in advance. There are also often same-day pre-show activities in the lower lobby—usually an art or movement project—all free.

Most shows run between two and six weeks, and performance typically take less than two hours. Booster seats are available.

If you like this sight, you may also like Puppetworks (#18).

EATS FOR KIDS Junior's (W. 45th St., tel. 212/302-2000) is one of the few tourist-oriented restaurants in Times Square that's well worth a visit. Although the prices are somewhat outrageous and the food merely decent, the cheesecake is the stuff of NYC legend. And the atmosphere is just as worthwhile—it hasn't changed much since the '50s, when it opened. (OK, the original location was in Brooklyn, but the spirit's the same.)

NEW YORK AQUARIUM

This aquarium is in every way a survivor. Despite a perpetual challenge to maintain and modernize itself—as well as a daunting mandate to rebuild and reopen in the wake of major damage wrought by Hurricane Sandy—this facility has always held its head high as the home to thousands of species of marine life, including Pacific walruses, giant sea turtles, sand-tiger sharks, and sea otters.

The beauty and grace of jellyfish have a way of transfixing kids that is often a revelation to parents—and the Alien Stingers exhibit doesn't disappoint, especially when kids encounter a jellyfish such as the flower hat, whose upturned green and purple stingers do make it resemble an alien creature.

Also popular are the predators in the 90,000-gallon tank that holds sharks, turtles, fish, and stingrays. Be sure to ask why the sharks don't eat their fellow roommates.

MAKE THE MOST OF YOUR TIME As of this writing the aquarium

had closed in order to repair damage from Hurricane Sandy; prior to that, the Aquatheater was undergoing renovations. With luck, you will be visiting a restored facility and seeing the sea lions in their new home. Check the website before you go to monitor the status of the aquarium's recovery and, above all, lend it your support by visiting once it is up and running.

Boardwalk at Surf Ave. and W. 8th St., Coney Island, Brooklyn
Subway: D, N to Coney Island/Stillwell Ave.; F, Q to W. 8th St.

Mar 30–May 24, 10–5 (5:30 weekends); May 26–Sept 3, 10–6 (7 weekends), Sept 4–Nov. 4, 10–5 (5:30 weekends); Nov 5–Mar 29, 10–4:30 daily

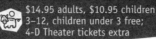 718/265-3474; www. nyaquarium.com

$14.95 adults, $10.95 children 3–12, children under 3 free; 4-D Theater tickets extra

 All ages

In Explore the Shore your family can stand under a 400-gallon tidal wave that crashes every 30 seconds. A Plexiglas hood keeps you dry, but the power of the sea may leave you breathless. Before heading out, be sure to visit the busy indoor touch pool (an outdoor one is also open in the summer) where volunteers assist kids eager to touch crabs and other creatures. As always, this is as good a reason as any to have your portable bottle of hand sanitizer at the ready.

If you like this sight, you may also like the Bronx Zoo (#65).

KEEP IN MIND A couple of 4-D movies, anywhere from 10 to 20 minutes long, may add to your experience if you are willing to spring for a Total Experience ticket or pay the extra $6 per person, per movie fee.

EATS FOR KIDS Assuming you didn't bring a picnic lunch (you can delve into a BYO picnic basket at tables in the aquarium), don't fancy eating at the indoor **Seaside Café,** and can resist the siren song of Coney Island's crinkle fries at **Nathan's** (1310 Surf Ave., tel. 718/946–2202), why not expand your experience with lunch in Brighton Beach? Restaurants like **Tatiana** (3152 Brighton 6th St., tel. 718/891–5151) share the neighborhood's Russian flavor. With an opulent over-the-top dining room and 20-page menu, kids are sure to find a few things they like.

NEW YORK BOTANICAL GARDEN

Kids don't get jazzed about plants or spend time debating the difference between a Japanese maple and ashleaf maple.

Being well aware of this, the NYBG wins kids over with attractions ranging from 10-minutes-of-distraction-so-you-take-a-quick-glance-at-those-orchids to entire kid-family areas that can fill up to an hour or more.

The Everett Children's Adventure Garden is an example of the latter. Good for 45–90 minutes, it's a magical garden full of mazes, larger-than-life flowers, water plants, and an indoor laboratory.

Check out the daily schedule of children's activities. There is usually one activity around growing, gardening, harvesting, or cooking aimed at children.

If you can secure some adult time, explore the magnificent 250 acres filled with 30,000 trees and 50 diverse gardens. A visit during spring and summer requires careful

MAKE THE MOST OF YOUR TIME

The botanical garden is less crowded on weekdays, except Wednesday, when admission is free (admission is also free Saturday 10 am to noon). A narrated tram tour lets you explore various places then reboard. Guided walks and audio tours are best suited to older children.

EATS FOR KIDS The indoor-outdoor **Garden Café** and the **Leon Levy Visitor Center Café** serve kid-pleasing comfort foods. Picnic tables are available at the Clay Family Picnic Pavilions, outside the Everett Children's Adventure Garden. Beyond the garden in Belmont, also called Arthur Avenue, try one of the many pizza parlors and Italian restaurants. **Dominick's** (2335 Arthur Ave., tel. 718/733–2807) and **Emilia's** (2331 Arthur Ave., tel. 718/367–5915) have inexpensive family-style Italian fare.

Bronx River Pkwy. at Fordham
Rd., Bronx
Subway: 4, B, D to Bedford Park

$10 adults, $5 students,
$2 children 2–12; Sa 10–11
and all day W free

T–Su, 10–6

718/817-8700; www.nybg.org

1 and up

planning to ensure that you can see at least four to five of your favorite areas, since all are in bloom: orchids, lilacs, tulips, the herb garden, and flowering cherry trees. A fall visit is so magnificent it practically substitutes for an upstate drive.

Coming during a seasonal festival can enhance your experience. The spring Cherry Blossom Festival is a welcome end to the cold weather, while the Edible Garden event (held in summer and early fall) celebrates locally grown foods. Booking in advance is advised.

Winter has its own appeal, thanks to the wildly popular Holiday Train Show, on from the end of November through mid-January. Families go inside the Enid A. Haupt Conservatory (greenhouse) to follow the path of a train traveling around a model of New York City complete with a mini Ellis Island, Statue of Liberty, and Radio City Music Hall. Avoid crowds by going early on a school day. Otherwise, prepare to spend at least an hour standing while filing through the exhibit.

If you like this sight, you may also like the Brooklyn Botanic Garden (#64).

KEEP IN MIND For a wonderful selection of gardening tools, toys, and plant-related items for children, visit The Kids Shop in the Children's Adventure Garden. The Gift Shop in the main retail area is also the place to take home a pint-sized pot for your child to plant at home. Consider bringing home a "please touch" plant for your garden. Lamb's ears, bee balm, lavender, and lemon balm all provide interesting textures, and the latter three are also aromatic when a child rubs its leaves.

In a renovated three-story firehouse built in 1904, you and your family can view one of the most comprehensive collections of fire-related art and artifacts from the 18th century to the present. Large firehouse doors, the housewatch (front desk) entrance, a stone floor, brass sliding pole, and hose tower remind visitors of the former home of Engine Company 30, its firefighters, rigs, and horses. The nonprofit museum operates in partnership with the New York City Fire Department, which owns the building and provides the collection. Kids five and up may be equally captivated by the firefighters who serve as tour guides.

Highlights for young children or future firefighters include getting a picture taken in a real NYC fireman's helmet and coat. Little ones will also enjoy spotting "Chief," the firehouse canine hero tucked away in his corner; while parents and older children, may appreciate the 9/11 Memorial Room, which honors the 343 New York City firefighters who died on September 11th, 2001. Permanent and temporary exhibitions chronicle the evolution of fire-fighting technology, beginning with the early bucket brigades. Carefully preserved

KEEP IN MIND If you're looking for a real climb-on experience, you're better off at the New York Transit Museum (#21). The fire trucks here are museum pieces, and exhibitions don't double as a hands-on playspace. Let your kids know what to expect to avoid disappointment.

278 Spring St., between Hudson and Varick Sts.
Subway: 1 to Houston St.; C, E to Spring St.

 Daily 10–5

 212/691–1303; www.
nycfiremuseum.org

 Suggested donation $8 adults,
$5 children 2–12

 2 and up

hand-operated, horse-drawn, and motorized equipment; toys; models; fire-engine lamps; presentation silver; oil paintings, prints, and photographs; "fire marks"; and folk art illuminate the traditions and lore of firefighting.

Preschoolers and early schoolers can learn why fires were a big problem in olden days and how bucket brigades worked. They'll be fascinated by how men pulled and pumped the early fire engines and how horses and dogs helped. They may also discover how firefighting changed as New York grew from a small village to a large city. Older kids can learn about the evolution of fire alarms, the duties of today's firefighters, and the teamwork involved in fighting fires. Don't forget to ask the guides how Dalmatian dogs became associated with firefighting.

If you like this sight, you may also like the New York City Police Museum (#25).

MAKE THE MOST OF YOUR TIME
The building can get crowded when group tours arrive, so call ahead to determine if any school trips are scheduled when you're planning to visit.

EATS FOR KIDS **Bubby's** (120 Hudson St., tel. 212/219–0666) is a 24/7 brunch spot that's popular with locals. Oversize muffins and sweet pancakes are kids' favorites, and there are board games available to help you while away the wait time.

NEW YORK CITY POLICE MUSEUM

W here else can you lock your kids in jail, let them play with guns, take them for a spin in a police cruiser, and help them fraternize with notorious criminals without someone calling Child Protective Services?

Actually, the guns are behind glass, there's no climbing on the cars, and the criminals are only in photos. But the spirit of Cops & Robbers make-believe is very much alive here, especially when kids step inside a genuine jail cell.

A collection of vehicles on the first floor should immediately pack appeal: picture a police cruiser, two motorcycles, bicycles, and a few scooters. Still more can be viewed during the annual summer car show, which features 50+ classic patrol cars from all 50 states, including Starsky & Hutch's Ford Gran Torino.

A relatively new addition to the museum is the Junior Officer Discovery Zone. It combines children's museum staples (namely a mock police car and a climbing structure that, in this case, resembles a police precinct) with opportunities to meet real officers, as

EATS FOR KIDS

For pub-style food, try **Stone Street Tavern** (52 Stone St., tel. 212/785–5658). Or head to **Adrienne's Pizza Bar** (54 Stone St., tel. 212/248–3838) for cheesy slabs of rectangle pizzas.

KEEP IN MIND This spot aims to engage, so curious and enthusiastic kids are welcome. Just remind your brood that one room requires a level of solemnity, The Hall of Heroes. The museum's most somber room contains the shields of every NYPD officer killed in the line of duty since the department began in 1845.

100 Old Slip (between Water and South Sts.)
Subway: 4, 5 to Bowling Green; 1 to South Ferry;
2, 3 to Wall St.; R, W to Whitehall St.

Suggested donation $8 adults,
$5 children; free under 2
and members of military and
police service

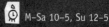
M–Sa 10–5, Su 12–5

212/480–3100; www.
nycpolicemuseum.org

8 and up

well as a very novel way to tire kids out: A fitness test sees how many times your child can run back and forth in 30 seconds.

To the Facebook generation, the adjacent telecommunications section—with its switchboard, pre-rotary-dial phones, even a telegraph—can seem quaint. After checking out police uniforms, go to the second-floor favorite, Vintage Weapons & Notorious Criminals. Meet America's favorite villains, from Benjamin "Bugsy" Siegel to Louise the Lump, and see weapons including Al Capone's famous Tommy Gun.

The top floor is dedicated to the permanent exhibit called 9/11 Remembered, which is simultaneously a tribute to those who helped and a disturbing reminder of the images and artifacts of destruction.

There are several annual events, often tied to holidays, where children can meet police officers, don uniforms, and try out their detective skills. Particularly memorable are the annual Halloween Party and Junior Detective Day. Check the calendar for specifics.

If you like this sight, you may also like the New York City Fire Museum (#26).

MAKE THE MOST OF YOUR TIME The museum
can be done in 30–90 minutes, depending on your kid's attachment to law enforcement. In addition to seeing the exhibits, leave some time to talk with museum staff. They're full of fun trivia. Ask nicely, and they'll share with you the answers to such puzzlers as, Why are police called cops? Who designed the Medal of Valor? Where can the Yankees logo be found in the museum and why?

NEW YORK HALL OF SCIENCE

The assumption here is that every child is born a scientist. The mission is merely to grow knowledge and keep the fires of curiosity burning bright.

And certainly this institution succeeds in making the basic principles of science easy and entertaining. Although kids 7+ will get the most out of the facility as a whole, there's enough to keep younger ones busy for a couple of hours.

The smallest kids, start at Preschool Place. This indoor playspace includes a magical two-story tree house hideaway that hosts regular shows and story times. There is plenty for young hands to safely do here: make block buildings, stage a puppet show, turn cranks. Best of all, there is a staff member blocking entry at all times, giving toddler-toting parents a moment's respite.

Older kids will love exhibits like Sports Challenge (and parents will love that it burns up their excess energy). In the Balance, Bounce, Climbing, Leap, Pitching, and Race challenges,

EATS FOR KIDS The on-site café has plenty of seats and a nice view of the play-ground, but the food is your typical dismal heat-lamp fare. A better option is **Corona Pizza** (5123 108th St., tel. 718/271–3736), a few blocks away. The slices here aren't brick-oven gourmet, but they're filling. More importantly, you'll be across the street from the **Lemon Ice King of Corona** (52-02 108th St., tel. 718/699–5133), a true Queens classic. Even in winter, kids get Italian ices in 30+ varieties as well as candy apples and other treats.

47-01 111th St., Flushing Meadows–
Corona Park, Flushing, Queens
Subway: 7 to 111th St.

$11 adults, $8
children 2–17; Science
Playground extra

July–Aug, M–F 9:30–5, Sa–Su 10–6; Sept–Mar,
Tu–Th 9:30–2, F 9:30–5, Sa–Su 10–6; Apr–June,
M–Th 9:30–2, Fri 9:30–5, Sa–Su 10–6

718/699-0005; www.
nyscience.org

2 and up, Science
Playground all ages

kids do a fitness activity that demonstrates a principle of physics, such as scaling an 8-foot climbing wall to learn about levers, throwing a fast ball to get a grasp of speed, trajectory, and spin, or surfing on a real board to understand more about their center of gravity).

Seeing the Light, meanwhile, spotlights the world of color, light, and perception through 80+ displays. Discover how the eye works, appear to fly via an antigravity mirror, or shrink and grow by walking across the Distorted Room.

In summer, going to the Science Playground (30,000 square feet of water, sand, slide, and science goodness) is a must. Unfortunately, they have a policy of only allowing people to do 90-minute sessions—keep that in mind with younger kids. Also keep in mind that unless you're buying a combo ticket, the Science Playground is $4 per child above the cost of general admission.

If you like this sight, you may also like the Liberty Science Center (#39).

MAKE THE MOST OF YOUR TIME

The Queens location makes it mercifully immune to the crowds Manhattan museums are plagued with. Even during the busiest times, the only real wait you'll experience is for the outdoor playground. This makes it an ideal escape from the holiday hordes.

KEEP IN MIND Students with 90% and above marks in both math and science can receive a free one-year Honors Membership to the museum, just another reason to hit the books. As for history, the Hall of Science is in Flushing Meadows–Corona Park, site of the 1939 and 1964 World's Fairs (its Unisphere is easily spotted from miles around). Also in the park are the Queens Zoo (#16) and the Queens Museum of Art (#17).

NEW-YORK HISTORICAL SOCIETY

ew Yorkers sometimes think their city is the center of the universe, and this museum only reinforces the argument. A cousin to the Museum of the City of New York across the park, it aims to show not only a slice of life through objects: It also strives to demonstrate just how far the city's influence reaches.

The rotating exhibits demonstrate this the most clearly. They don't focus solely on possessions or people with an obvious connection to the storied metropolis. They focus instead on topics, people, or events whose lives or outcomes were influenced by their connections to the city. Two recent ones (Grateful Dead and Lincoln) show the role it played in each subject's popular and political ascent, respectively. Far from stuffy, both exhibits are easy to digest in a 10-minute walkthrough.

KEEP IN MIND

The gift shop has many New York–themed items. So it's a good place to stock up if you're in the market for affordable, one-of-a-kind souvenirs.

EATS FOR KIDS

Zabar's (2245 Broadway, tel. 212/787–2000) is the Upper West Side's go-to shop for classic NYC stapes like bagels, lox, and herring. You can also get sandwiches, cheeses, and their legendary Russian coffee cake. Bring it to Riverside Park for a picnic overlooking the Hudson River or to eat while playing at Hippo Playground. **Sarabeth's** (423 Amsterdam Ave., tel. 212/496–6280) is a crowd-pleaser, especially for brunch, when you can sample French toast, red omelets, or delectable pumpkin muffins.

170 Central Park West, between 76th and 77th Sts.
Subway: 1 to 79th St.; B, C to 81st St.

 $15 adults, $10 students, $5 children 5–13

T-Th and Sa 10–6, F 10–8, Su 11–5

212/873–3400; www.nyhistory.org

 7 and up

The relatively new DiMenna Children's History Museum on the lower level (targeted at children eight to 13) uses games, kiosks, touch-screens, and other interactive exhibits to introduce kids to major (and not so major) figures in history. The twist is that you meet those folks as young people who have yet to gain prominence. Witness Alexander Hamilton when he was a student coming to NYC for college, or Esteban Bellan, a New Yorker from Cuba, who became the first Latin American to play major-league baseball.

The Henry Luce Center on the fourth floor is worth a visit, too. It displays such noteworthy historical pieces as a Queen Anne roundabout chair that kids will learn has a flip-up seat with access to a toilet. Also on display is a full-size plaster model of Abe Lincoln's head, used as a study by sculptor Daniel Chester French for the Lincoln Memorial

If you like this sight, you might like the Guggenheim (#44).

MAKE THE MOST OF YOUR TIME Throughout
the day, the ground-floor theater runs a worthwhile documentary, *New York Story*, that manages to sum up the history of the city in a mere 18 minutes.

NEW YORK PUBLIC LIBRARY

If there were an award for Most Underused NYC Resource, this would win. With a plethora of family programs throughout the library's 87 branches, dozens of child-centric reading rooms, and visits by celebrities, authors, and celebrity-authors, a visit to the NYPL should be at the top of your list. And you don't even need a local library card to participate.

The Main Library—on 42nd and 5th, guarded by its two iconic lion statues—is huge by Midtown standards and stocked with a collection so big you'd have to extend your visit by a few years to read every book. Not only does it have a Children's Center, it also contains a permanent Winnie-the-Pooh exhibit. For a first birthday present, Christopher Robin Milne (A.A. Milne's son) was given a small teddy bear. Soon he was given four more friends (Eeyore, Piglet, Kanga, and Tigger). His father decided to use them in a bedtime story, and the rest, as we say, is history. The library displays all of them here.

Other branches with custom-designed children's centers are well worth a visit, especially on inclement days. Visit St. Agnes (Upper West Side), Mulberry Street (a former chocolate

EATS FOR KIDS If family-style portions of pastas and chicken suit the brood you have in tow then **Tony's Di Napoli** (147 W. 43rd St., tel. 212/221–0100) is dependable and has become expert at serving quickly. While you don't necessarily need to come to NYC to eat at **Panera Bread** (452 5th Ave., tel. 212/938–6950), New Yorkers are actually quite happy to have them here (finally) and this branch is particularly spacious and pleasant.

Main branch: 476 5th Ave. at 42nd St.
Subway: 1, 2, 3 to 42nd St./Broadway; A, C to 42nd St./8th
Ave.; D, B, F, M to 42nd St./6th Ave.; 4, 5, 6 to Grand Central

 Free

 Varies by location

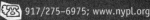 917/275-6975; www.nypl.org

2 and up

factory and a great place to read Dr. Seuss's *And To Think I Saw It on Mulberry Street*), and the brand-new Battery Park City Library.

There's a fun activity for children almost every day of the week. For the youngest kids, there are usually morning story times. For school-age children in the K–6 category, the offerings expand greatly to include arts and crafts, computer classes, movies, game sessions (involving both traditional board games and modern video games), knitting, reading aloud, karaoke, gardening, the list goes on . . .

Special events (called Touring Programs) are limited in location and regularity, often repeating fewer than four times. Recent events have included Mario Batali reading to kids, a performance of Czech fairytales complete with marionettes, Mad Science workshops, book making, stamp making, and face painting.

If you like this sight, you may also like the New-York Historical Society (#23).

MAKE THE MOST OF YOUR TIME Go to the website
to search for weekly recurring events and special happenings. Check nearby locations and also those slightly farther afield, as a quick subway ride may be all that stands between you and something free to do every day.

KEEP IN MIND
Along with Starbucks and chain bookstores, most library branches have restrooms and are a good place duck into when you need to make a pit stop.

NEW YORK TRANSIT MUSEUM

With its cut-away buses, vintage subway cars, and all sorts of levers and steering wheels that kids can operate, the Transit Museum is about as interactive as it can be. In fact, even youngsters who aren't obsessed with trains, buses, and other wheeled things will love coming here to jump into "traffic." It's a whole lot of fun. Just be warned: You may have to spend the rest of your trip listening to your little tykes sing "The Wheels on the Bus" in an endless loop.

Housed in a decommissioned 1936 Brooklyn subway station, the museum gives kids a tactile understanding of the history of public transportation in New York City and beyond. Expect to see a century's worth of transit memorabilia, including 19 restored subway cars (they span a 60-year period from 1904 to 1964) plus antique turnstiles, a working signal tower, and a surface transportation room.

KEEP IN MIND If you can't make it out to Brooklyn, the Annex in Grand Central is good for a quick, free visit providing a glimpse at New York City's transportation life. There's only one exhibit, but it usually captivates kids. Recent ones have included a holiday mechanical train show and The Subway in Film. The shop is what most people come for, with unique souvenirs like T-shirts displaying a favorite subway line, authentic subway artifacts like signs or tokens, and just about everything imprinted with the subway map (shower curtain anyone?).

Boerum Pl. and Schermerhorn St., Brooklyn Heights
Subway: 2, 3, 4, 5 to Borough Hall; R to Court St.; A, C, G
to Hoyt-Schermerhorn St.; A, C, F, R to Jay St./MetroTech

 T–F 10–4, Sa–Su 11–5

 718/694–1600; www.mta.
info/museum

$7 adults, $5 children 3–17

2 and up

There are weekly children's programs where guides lead their young charges in an art, storytelling, film, or movement activity covering popular topics like tokens, bridges, subway tiles, trains, or maps.

For a real thrill, and to make the past and present collide, conclude your visit with one of their community tours or nostalgia rides. Take a vintage train to a popular destination like Coney Island or the Rockaways. Tours (for children five and up) pull the curtain back on the transit system and important transport-related places providing an insider's view of things like the Westchester Yards (the 14,000-square-foot subway maintenance shop), Staten Island's oddities, and South Ferry as seen through the eyes of the author of *Manhattan: A Natural History of New York City*.

If you like this sight, you may also like the *Intrepid* Sea, Air & Space Museum (#41).

MAKE THE MOST OF YOUR TIME
Go at off-peak times (Tuesdays or early afternoons, when there are no school groups), or else your kids may get stuck waiting a while for their turn to be the "bus driver."

EATS FOR KIDS An ode to British fish-and-chips fare, the **ChipShop** (129 Atlantic Ave., tel. 718/855–7775) has an entire menu for kids, including mac-and-cheese for the seafood-squeamish. Ribs and shrimp are among the pickings at **The Soul Spot** (302 Atlantic Ave., tel. 866/945–8425), a neighborhood place that blends soul food with Caribbean flair. Curried goat is available for the adventurous.

PROSPECT PARK

Central Park gets all the attention, but this park, which shares the same designers (Olmsted and Vaux), is Brooklyn's pride and joy. Its 585 acres are equally satisfying for a 10-minute dash or a day-long excursion.

Visiting families should hit these highlights:

The 1912 carousel ($2 per ride, April–October) has 51 horses, a lion, a giraffe, and a deer, as well as two dragon-drawn chariots, all brought to life by master carver Charles Carmel.

The Prospect Park Audubon Center lets kids dive into nature with sculptural birds and squirrels they can pose in. It's home to great children's programs, too, including bird-watching, nature crafts, and, in summer, periodic Twilight Tours, where kids can spot bats and other nocturnal creatures. This is also where, May through October, you pick up the Electric Boat Tours of Brooklyn's only freshwater lake ($10 adults, $5 children 4–13).

KEEP IN MIND
Visiting families with more time might want to tack on a trip to Prospect Park Zoo (#19), nearby Brooklyn Botanic Garden (#64) or the Brooklyn Museum (#61).

MAKE THE MOST OF YOUR TIME
Prospect Park's attractions are very spread out, not concentrated in one area like Central Park's. Either pick one or two attractions to do in an hour or so, or plan on spending at least half a day here. Also note that there are no pedicabs; you'll be walking most of the way yourself!

Eastern Pkwy. and Grand Army Plaza, Brooklyn
Subway: F, G, Q, S, B to Prospect Park; 2, 3 to Grand Army Plaza

 Daily sunrise–1 AM

718/965–8999 information line, 718/
965–8969 permits, 718/287–3400
Audubon Center; www.prospectpark.org

Free; some attractions charge

 All ages

Every Sunday (2 PM–dusk) conga drummers continue a tradition started in 1968. Musicians and dancers gather for a weekly drumming circle in, you guessed it, Drummer's Grove (near the Parkside Avenue subway stop) and kids are encouraged to join in dancing or drumming. If you're inclined to try the latter, people will kindly loan their instruments.

Kensington Stables offers lessons and pony rides every day from 10 AM to sunset. Advance reservations are recommended, but you might get lucky as a walk-up ($3 for a pony ride; $47 per hour group lesson; $52 semiprivate; $57 private lessons or $34 per half hour).

Lefferts House (built in the 1800s by a Dutch family) takes kids back in time 200 years via traditional toys, tools, and games.

Wollman Rink (Brooklyn's only outdoor rink) is open for ice skating mid-November through March. The rest of the year families can rent pedal boats for touring the lake.

If you like this sight, you may also like Central Park (#57).

EATS FOR KIDS To the west of Prospect Park is Park Slope, otherwise known as Stroller Land to New Yorkers. This area is dominated by young families, which means restaurants here welcome little diners and cater to their tastes. Fifth Avenue is the hood's main drag, and you'll be spoiled for choice. Reliable regulars include Italian classics at **Al Di La Trattoria** (248 5th Ave., tel. 718/638–8888) or the **ChipShop** (129 Atlantic Ave., tel. 718/855–7775) for British fish-and-chips.

PROSPECT PARK ZOO

The Wildlife Conservation Society (parent organization to the zoos in Central Park, Queens, Prospect Park, and the Bronx, as well as the New York Aquarium) keeps its various venues distinct by distributing different animals in each property. Naturally, the biggest mammals are mostly restricted to the Bronx Zoo and aquatic animals call the Aquarium home. The smaller animals, or animals requiring less living space, can be found scattered in the five boroughs. (With the exception of sea lions, which seem to be everywhere!)

Go to the Prospect Park Zoo (which has 12 acres of naturalistic habitats) to observe kangaroos and wallabies that you won't see elsewhere. Both are found on Discovery Trail. Activities for kids to do here include burrowing in Plexiglas-topped tunnels, popping up next to a prairie dog, or leap-frogging across giant lily pads to goose nests. In the 2,500-foot aviary at trail's end, look for free-flying African birds and peacocks.

The Animal Lifestyles building is home to air, water, and land animals, including reptiles, amphibians, fish, birds, and small mammals. The standout is the 4,500-square-foot

EATS FOR KIDS When the line is bearable (midweek) and the kids aren't starving, walk the three blocks to **Tom's Diner** (782 Washington Ave., tel. 718/636–9738), no relation to Suzanne Vega. Load up on carbs and calories with fluffy pancakes, milk shakes, and other diner food done right.

450 Flatbush Ave., Prospect Park, Brooklyn
Subway: B,Q to Prospect Park

 718/399-7339; www.prospectparkzoo.org

 $8 ages 13 and up,
$5 children 3–12

 Mar 31–Nov 4, M–F 10–5, Sa–Su
10–5:30; Nov 5–Mar 29, Daily
10–4:30

All ages

hamadryas baboon exhibit. You're only a thin sheet of glass away from these primates (the contrast between their furry bodies and bare, bright pink rumps invariably makes kids giggle). Don't be surprised if a friendly baboon approaches the glass to study you back.

In the Barnyard & Garden area, youngsters can peek into the chicken coop or come face to face with farm animals like sheep, cows, and alpacas. Little ones seem to particularly enjoy the equally little miniature horses and pygmy goats. For an aquatic alternative, check out the California sea lions as they frolic noisily in a rocky California coast–like environment. They are fed daily at 11:30, 2, and 4.

If you like this sight, you may also like the Queens Zoo (#16).

KEEP IN MIND
It's always wise to wipe young hands frequently during visits here. Carry wet wipes or dampened washcloths in ziplock bags for quick hand swiping before snack time or lunch.

MAKE THE MOST OF YOUR TIME
The location of this zoo is ideal for a day out with the kids. On arrival check the daily schedule for the times of free Keeper Chats, Highlight Tours and other kid-friendly activities. When you're done, the Brooklyn Museum (#61), Brooklyn Children's Museum (#62), Brooklyn Botanic Garden (#64) and Brooklyn Library are within a few minutes' walk away.

PUPPETWORKS

18

S ome kids yearn to hear live actors belt out show tunes on Broadway. Others prefer their entertainment with a few strings attached. If yours fall into the second group, this is the place to be.

For more than 35 years the Puppetworks, Inc., under the artistic direction of Nicolas Coppola, has been known throughout the country for it's mostly marionette productions. In 1987 the troupe opened a permanent 75-seat theater in a Park Slope (Brooklyn) storefront, next to the Puppetworks workshop. This informal, family-friendly venue presents daily performances of children's literary classics, with weekdays reserved for groups (20 or more).

Traditional puppet theater favorites might include *Pinocchio*, *The Prince & The Magic Flute*, or *Hansel & Gretel*. And each production is faithful to its source, whether that's fairy tales, folk tales, or children's literature.

MAKE THE MOST OF YOUR TIME

Age recommendations for each performance are listed on the website, along with a schedule of shows, dates, and times. The performances here are interactive, with nothing scary, so there's no need to worry about nightmares.

EATS FOR KIDS For comfort food and diner delights (think fluffy Belgian waffles, bacon-wrapped meat loaf, and stick-to-your ribs barbecue ribs), visit **Dizzy's** (511 9th St., tel. 718/499–1966). **Tomato and Basil** (226 4th Ave., tel. 718/596–8855) is perfect for pizza, and **Miriam** (79 5th Ave., tel. 718/622–2250) is delicious for Israeli cuisine or eggs and omelets anytime.

338 6th Ave., at 4th St., Brooklyn
Subway: F, G to 7th Ave.

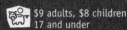 $9 adults, $8 children
17 and under

 Varies by show

 718/965-3391; www.
puppetworks.org

 3-12

On average, shows feature 13 puppet characters per, though some have had as many as 68. Amazingly, just two puppeteers are responsible for each performance (and you thought you had your hands full!). Professionally designed sets with distinctive painted backdrops and intricate puppet costumes give the feeling of a scaled-down Broadway show. At the end of many performances a professional puppeteer will bring out one of the beautiful, hand-carved "stars" to show to the audience, giving a brief behind-the-scenes or, more accurately, above-the-strings talk about the workings of a puppet theater. Children are encouraged to ask questions. The walls of the theater also display close to 100 marionettes that appeared in past performances, though many are reused and recostumed.

If you like this sight, you may also like the New Victory Theater (#29).

KEEP IN MIND Since 1976, when Macy's built a gingerbread puppet theater for Puppetworks at its flagship department store, more than 50,000 children and their families have attended the annual Puppetworks Christmas performances. Bring yours to the eighth floor of Macy's Herald Square (Broadway at 34th St., tel. 212/695-4400) and start a new tradition. The holiday-theme performances are given 10 times daily and cost only a few dollars.

Families heading to the New York Hall of Science should absolutely make a stop here. While the majority of the museum is fine, the real draw is a miraculous miniature city—The Panorama.

Imagine giving your kids unlimited Legos, a 10,000-square-foot table, turning on Google maps (street view), then throwing in a little electricity, and you'll begin to picture what's on display here. It is simply the most magnificent replica of New York City you will see anywhere.

Laid out on a massive platform, the Panorama is an architectural model of the five boroughs of the city, and every single building (before 1992) is represented. Yes, every single one. From the grand (like the Empire State) to the teeny (think three-floor town houses), they're all here—895,000 individual structures in total.

Most of the other civic and natural features are included as well, among them bridges, parks, rivers, roads, tugboats, stadiums, and more. The Panorama was conceived by NYC's

KEEP IN MIND The best bargain in Manhattan real estate is in Queens. For $50 you can "own" any apartment you like on the Panorama. You will get a deed to the "property" (which makes a cute souvenir) and be acknowledged for at least five years. Bigger donations allow you to own icons like the Brooklyn Bridge. All funds go toward the maintenance, modernization, and upkeep of the Panorama.

Flushing Meadows Corona Park, Corona, Queens
Subway: 7 to Mets-Willets Point

 $8 adults, $4 children
5 and up

 W–Su 12–6

718/592-9700; www.queensmuseum.org

1 and up

"master builder" and preeminent urban planner, Robert Moses, who commissioned it for the 1964 World's Fair with a contract stipulating that there be no more than a 1% margin of error between reality and model—talk about pressure! One hundred people working for Lester Associates built it originally, a task which took three years. The same company then updated it in 1992, changing 60,000 structures. The coolest change was made in 2006, allowing it to be displayed in different light conditions to highlight different buildings or areas and to re-create sounds of the city. Other details add to the realism, like the Lilliputian planes that take off and land at the airport, traveling along a transparent string.

On weekends the museum runs family drop-in art workshops (not connected to the Panorama).

If you like this sight, you may like Historic Richmond Town (#42).

EATS FOR KIDS
Empanada Cafe (56–27 Van Doren St., tel. 718/592-7288) is known as the "United Nations of Empanadas," with more than 20 varieties including organic and vegetarian options. The prices can't be beat (most are under $2).

MAKE THE MOST OF YOUR TIME On the second Sunday of every month, the museum hosts MetLife Second Sundays for Families. Recent activities, which typically tie into existing exhibits, have included meeting the collaborative team behind the Curse of Bigness exhibit and seeing a Toy Theater in action.

QUEENS ZOO

16

Just as the Bronx Zoo's majesty lies in its large size, this zoo's charm comes from intimacy—making it easily doable in under two hours. The compact layout, dearth of crowds, integrated climbing and play structures, impeccably clean petting zoo, and (in summer) easy access to a carousel, paddleboat lake, and fountain, make it a favorite for time-constrained families or those with small children.

There's only one circular path to follow, so it's almost impossible to get lost. Two big benefits are the proximity you get to the animals (while still giving them relatively large living spaces) and the well-chosen, unusual selection of critters kids won't normally see up close (owls, two bald eagles, and a mountain lion among them). Along the path there are plenty of structures specifically designed for children's play, including a balance beam, climbing pyramid, and Conservation Stations, where kids learn tips on saving the earth through interactive questions and games.

KEEP IN MIND

Among the other zoo animals in the Great Plains section is Otis, a coyote rescued from Central Park in 1999. He now safely resides here, away from cross-town yellow cabs.

A definite favorite here is the spacious farm animals section that doubles as a petting zoo. Come in spring and you just might see some newborn lambs.

MAKE THE MOST OF YOUR TIME If you're visiting on a weekend and want to take a quiet break with your preschooler, the Discovery Center is a comfy place to hang out with books, games, and a crafts station. Zoo educators are typically on hand to field questions as well supervise special weekend activities.

53-51 111th St., Flushing Meadows–
Corona Park, Flushing, Queens
Subway: 7 to 111th St.

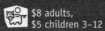 $8 adults,
$5 children 3–12

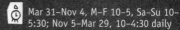 Mar 31–Nov 4, M–F 10–5, Sa–Su 10–
5:30; Nov 5–Mar 29, 10–4:30 daily

718/271-1500; www.queenszoo.com

All ages

Highlights of a visit here include:

Great Plains: With giant bison, a coyote, and a pronghorn antelope that can run 55 mph, it captures that "home on the range" quality.

Aviary: This geodesic dome designed by Buckminster Fuller for the 1964 World's Fair, is now home to ducks, turkeys, porcupines, cardinals, and egrets.

South American Trail: The adorable pudu particularly likes visitors and will often come right up to the glass to interact with kids. See if yours can spot the bear hiding in the trees.

Sea lion feedings: These happen every day at 11:15, 2, and 4. On weekends the Discovery Center, filled with books, games, a microscope, fossils, and a craft station, is open from noon to 4.

If you like this sight, you may also like the Staten Island Zoo (#8).

EATS FOR KIDS Feed your animal appetite at the cafeteria, overlooking the sea lions' pool. Or, for a light bite of Greek food, try the **Omonia Café** (32-20 Broadway, Astoria, tel. 718/274–6650). The cake for the movie *My Big Fat Greek Wedding* was created here.

RADIO CITY MUSIC HALL

To get behind the scenes of the lavish art deco palace that the high-kicking Rockettes call home, you'll want to take the Stage Door Tour. Along the way you'll learn about this landmark, the brainchild of theatrical impresario S.L. "Roxy" Rothafel. Radio City was the first building in the Rockefeller Center complex, and it was the world's largest indoor theater in 1932. In 1999 it was renovated to the tune of $70 million. Tours showcase the building's technological capabilities as well as its history. Luminaries such as Frank Sinatra, Ella Fitzgerald, and Sammy Davis Jr. have graced this stage, as have contemporary acts like FUN and the gang from *Glee*.

To whet your appetite, here are some amazing Radio City facts: the shimmering gold curtain is the largest theatrical curtain on earth. The mighty Wurlitzer organ, built in 1932, has two consoles, each weighing 2½ tons. Its pipes, some of which are 32 feet tall, are housed in 11 rooms. Look up and you can see a 24-carat gold-leaf ceiling glistening 60 feet above

KEEP IN MIND In 1979, to save the Music Hall from the wrecking ball, the program format was changed from films and stage shows to live concerts, television specials, and events. The *Radio City Christmas Spectacular*, *Blue's Clues*, *Dora the Explorer*, and adult and kids' concerts play to sold-out crowds throughout the year. You must typically purchase a ticket for children two and older for performances here; however, for some kid-centric shows, all youngsters one and older require a ticket, even if they plan to sit in your lap.

1260 6th Ave., at 50th St.
Subway: B, D, F to Rockefeller Center/
50th St.

212/465-6080 tours; 866/
858-0008 tickets (through
Ticketmaster); www.radiocity.com

Tour $23.70 adults,
$18.75 children 12
and under

Tours daily 11–3 every half hr

7 and up

you. For the record, the Music Hall contains over 25,000 lightbulbs inside; outside, the marquee is a block long and uses more than 6 miles of red and blue neon.

The Stage Door Tour also includes a visit to the private apartment of founder Roxy Rothafel and a stop in the costume shop, which contains outfits worn during the *Radio City Christmas Spectacular*. Your tour group will also meet a real member of the Radio City Rockettes, who will share some of the company's history. One-hour tours depart from the main lobby at the corner of Sixth Avenue and 50th Street.

Even if you don't take the tour, consider catching a stage show here and see all that technological wizardry at work.

If you like this sight, you may also enjoy the NBC Studios Tour (#30).

MAKE THE MOST OF YOUR TIME
Visiting Radio City Music Hall during the winter months is magical. Combine your trip with walking around or ice-skating at Rockefeller Center (#13), browsing at F.A.O. Schwarz (#48), or ogling the holiday windows along Fifth Avenue.

EATS FOR KIDS With the plethora of office workers around here, it's an ideal place to do as the locals do—get lunch from one of the food trucks! Several trucks and carts around 53rd Street and Sixth Avenue serve anything from authentic German sausage to whoopie pies. **Moshe's Falafel** (46th St. and 6th Ave.) has been ranked one of the best by the local press, and with three falafels for under $4, it's a steal.

RIPLEY'S BELIEVE IT OR NOT!

A list of random things displayed here—a lock of Elvis Presley's hair, a slab of the Berlin Wall, a hissing cockroach—reads like a scavenger hunt one has little hope of completing.

In a way, that sums up the mission of Robert Ripley. For more than 40 years, this cartoonist moonlighting as a collector tracked down artifacts that were unbelievably hard to find, and discovered people and creatures and customs that were hard to believe.

The result of his exertion—aside from a hugely popular series of cartoons and, later, books—was that many of these items found their way into 30+ Ripley's "Odditoriums" around the world, including the Times Square flagship.

According to Ripley's, every Odditorium displays (believe it or not) different items. The only recurring ones are re-created models of superlative finds—the world's tallest, shortest, fattest, etc. But kids won't necessarily care whether they're looking at a real artifact or reproduction. Take the wooden gallows, for instance. Pull the wooden lever beside

EATS FOR KIDS

Of your many, many burger options nearby, **Schnipper's Quality Kitchen** (620 8th Ave., tel. 212/921-2400) is one of the better ones. And years of doing the same thing have not dulled the crispy goodness at **John's Pizzeria** (260 W. 44th Street, tel. 212/391-7560).

MAKE THE MOST OF YOUR TIME

You should be able to knock off the two floors of Ripley's 20-odd galleries in under two hours, and while the Laser Maze—a timed trip through a maze requiring you to dodge green lasers—is included in admission, it may prove too intimidating for kids under six. If you still have an hour to kill afterwards you could be magnanimous and take the brood to **Toys"R"Us** (1514 Broadway at 44th St., tel. 646/366-8800) where you might be able to forestall a toy purchase by treating everyone to a ride on the 60-foot indoor Ferris wheel ($4 per person).

234 West 4th St., bet. 7th and 8th Aves.
Subway: 1, 2, 3, N, Q, R, 7, S to Times
Square; A, C, E to 42nd St./8th Ave.

212/398-3133;
www.ripleysnewyork.com

$33 adults, $25 children
4–12; includes general
admission and laser race

Daily 9 AM–1 AM

5 and up

it, and what appears to be the bottom half of a hanged man noisily bangs down and dangles.
Not real, but more entertaining with every pull.

Then consider the display of two dozen shrunken heads. What makes them interesting isn't that
the heads are, in fact, real, but that the museum gets kids thinking about the process. Posted
on the wall nearby is a head-shrinking how-to that involves stewing the head in a berry-herb
broth—but not before removing the scalp from the skull and reshaping the head, of course.

And that hissing live hissing cockroach? Several from Madagascar are kept behind glass
here. Kids have the opportunity to get up close by ducking under the display and sticking
their heads into an enclosed dome that protrudes into the cockroaches' case. Really,
what more can a kid ask for in a museum?

If you like this sight, you may also like Madame Tussauds Wax Museum (#37).

KEEP IN MIND Ripley's has embraced the "night at the museum"
trend with an overnight package (from $129 per child, with an adult chaper-
one required for every party of one to four kids). It includes the laser race, a
scavenger hunt, a movie, and other activities, along with dinner and breakfast.
This outing is appropriate for kids 6–17.

ROCKEFELLER CENTER AND THE ICE RINK

The price is outrageous, and the wait ranges from unpleasant to awful (depending on weather). But once you actually get to ice-skate under the golden statue of Prometheus while that gorgeous 80-plus-foot tree twinkles in the background, all is forgiven.

The experience is nothing short of breathtaking. And when you think of how your kids will be able to say "we skated there!" every time they see a movie set in New York City during the winter holidays, it becomes worth it to join the rite of passage that other families consider their holiday tradition.

Truth be told, it's really not all that bad, especially if you go during the lower traffic times (early mornings and weekdays before 5 PM or so). Going before the holiday season (from October until the end of November) is not only much less crowded, it's cheaper, with lower rates and occasional bargains. In past seasons they have offered a deal where noontime skaters pay $5 (rentals extra).

KEEP IN MIND Other great spots for a twirl on the ice are the Lasker and Wollman Memorial rinks (*see* Central Park, #57); Chelsea Piers' Sky Rink (tel. 212/336–6100); and Brooklyn's Wollman Rink (*see* Prospect Park, #20), not to be confused with the Wollman Memorial Rink in Central Park.

Bordered by 47th and 52nd Sts. and 5th and 7th Aves.; ice rink, between 49th and 50th Sts. and 5th and 6th Aves. Subway: B, D, F, V to 47–50th Sts./Rockefeller Center; N, R to 49th St.; 6 to 51st St.; 1 to 50th St.

212/332–7654 rink, 212/332–7655 lessons, 212/698–2000 Top of the Rock; www. rockefellercenter.com, www.topoftherocknyc.com

Skating early Jan–Apr and mid-Oct–early Nov $20 adults, $12 children under 11, skate rental $10; early Nov–early Jan $25 adults, $15 children under 11, $10 skate rental

 Skating early Nov–Apr 7 AM–12 AM; mid-Oct–early Nov 8:30 AM–12 AM

2 and up

Sessions are 1½ hours on a first-come, first-served basis. Skate and locker rentals, season passes and multi-ticket books, lessons, and group rates are all available, as are birthday parties with skate admissions, rental, and refreshments (January–April). During summer the rink turns into the Rink Bar, serving cocktails and bar bites. Children are admitted, but the atmosphere is far more for adults.

After hitting the ice (not literally, we hope!), set your sights high at Top of the Rock. The Rockefeller Center's six-level observatory is often considered a better alternative to the Empire State Building. Floor-to-ceiling windows provide eye-popping views of city landmarks.

If you like this sight, you may also like Central Park (#57).

EATS FOR KIDS
Dine at the **Rink Café and Bar,** open in summer 11–11, or the **Rock Center Café** (tel. 212/332–7620) year-round. **Bouchon Bakery** (1 Rockefeller Plaza, tel. 212/782–3890) serves quick sandwiches and treats.

MAKE THE MOST OF YOUR TIME Monday through Thursday, lunchtime skating is a bargain at $5. The same can't be said for Top of the Rock (tickets $17.50 for adults, $11.25 for children 6–12). But with great views, timed entries, and no lines, it's worth the price. Other things to keep families amused here include the NBC Studios Tour (#30) and popular kid-oriented shops like Nintendo World (tel. 646/459–0800) and the Lego Store (tel. 212/245–5973).

RUBIN MUSEUM

Telling kids you're going to see Himalayan art is the world's biggest buzzkill. Even families sporting "Free Tibet" stickers on their VWs don't get excited about the idea of shuffling through exhibitions with titles like The Nepalese Legacy in Tibetan Painting.

But don't let lofty language keep you from the enchanting tales your kids can uncover, like the one about the Tiger Rider who gave up his kingdom to be with an outcast woman, only to be asked to return and rule again; or the Dog Lover who left a luxurious paradise to live in a cave with his beloved canine companion, only to have her turn into a beautiful woman.

The treasures here are stunning, and older kids will appreciate the artistry that went into making the jewelry and figurines (magnifying glasses hang on hooks in case anyone wants a closer look at the details). The draw for younger kids, though, will be the second-floor Gateway to Himalayan Art exhibit, where one wall is dedicated to showing how some of the artwork was created, start to finish. Kids will see the progression, from the beeswax molds for the metal to little chisels and hammers used for finishing the pieces.

KEEP IN MIND

A few times a year the museum holds Family Days, with a slew of family-friendly activities. And on October 2, the anniversary of the museum's founding, they host a day-long art and peacemaking extravaganza known as the International Day of Non-Violence.

MAKE THE MOST OF YOUR TIME

The galleries can be done in 20–45 minutes, perfect for little ones' attention spans. The easiest way to tackle them is to take the elevator to the sixth floor and work your way down the stairway, floor by floor. The second floor is where you'll likely linger the longest, as it offers the most behind-the-scenes approach to the artwork. When you're done, look for enchanting, affordable items—like Buddha water-painting kits and bead bracelets—in the museum gift shop.

150 W. 17th St.
Subway: A, C, E to 14th St.; N, R, Q, 4, 5, 6
to 14th St. Union Sq.; 1 to 18th St.

212/620–5000; www.rmanyc.org

$10 adult, $5 students
13 and up; free F 6–10;
family workshops extra

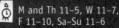
M and Th 11–5, W 11–7,
F 11–10, Sa–Su 11–6

All ages

Also on the second floor is the Tibetan Shrine Room. The actual room is roped off and diligently overseen by a museum guard, but it's worthwhile to try to force a moment of reflection on your kids as they take in the music and lit candles of the shrine; audio wands dangling from the barricade explain the story behind it.

Drop-in family workshops help make the museum's art even more accessible. Yak Packers Early Childhood Artmaking (Wednesday and Thursday mornings) includes an hour of craft activities and staff-led trips to the gallery for kids two to four. Family Art Labs (the second Saturday of the month) include a two-hour session of similar activities for kids five and older. The $16 workshops include the price of general admission.

If you like this sight, you may also like the New-York Historical Society (#23).

EATS FOR KIDS Save your appetite for the outstanding fare at **City Bakery** (3 W. 18th St., tel. 212/366–1414). After an obligatory-but-delicious lunch of vegetables, salads, sandwiches, or other salad-bar staples, it's time to reward yourself with a face-sized chocolate-chip cookie, thick-as-mud hot chocolate, or the signature pretzel croissants—a France-meets-the-Fatherland treat that's flaky, dense, sweet, buttery, and salty all at once.

SNUG HARBOR

Everyone loves to take the Staten Island Ferry, but 99.9% of its out-of-town passengers used to just turn around, get back on, and immediately return to Manhattan.

Then Staten Island got smart. A few years back someone decided that visitors would venture here more often if the main attractions were easier to reach. This 83-acre former retirement center for seamen was restored, and now it's home to many kid-friendly institutions.

Start at the Staten Island Children's Museum. Ideal for those under seven, it offers a good balance between indoor, outdoor, and hands-on activities. Favorite areas include the Block Harbor (play on a pirate ship), Bugs & Other Insects (see bees working or move into an "ant apartment"), and a real stage (put on costumes and perform). During warmer months the Sea of Boats outdoor playground is a small water-play area. Most days they have one or two interactive programs for kids to participate in. Often animals from the Staten Island Zoo will come visit, or kids will be called upon to do a science, cooking, or art project.

KEEP IN MIND The Staten Island Museum (75 Stuyvesant Pl., tel. 718/727–1135) is reputed to be moving here, but no one is willing to set a date for that event. Until then, if you have time before the ferry, stop in on your way to Snug Harbor or back to the ferry landing. (It's across the street from the terminal). More eccentric-old-mad-scientist's-collection than museum, this is really a grouping of curiosities. There are some paintings and plenty of local interest items, but what kids will beg to see is the display of fluorescent rocks that glow when the room goes dark.

Snug Harbor Cultural Center, 1000 Richmond Terr., Staten Island
Subway: To Staten Island Ferry terminal, 1 to South Ferry or 4, 5
to Bowling Green or R to Whitehall

 Varies by attraction

718/448–2500;
www.snug-harbor.org

 Varies by attraction

1 and up

The Noble Maritime Museum is a lesser-known attraction that has recently been renovated with a strong eye toward visiting families. Named for John A. Noble, an artist and lover of everything maritime, this spot allows kids to adopt a sailor's persona for a few hours. Don't miss the tugboat cabin (where kids get to be captain), Noble's houseboat studio (offering a look at life on a teeny vessel), the Crosswalk Gallery (where objects there have been intentionally placed lower and wall text is written with a younger audience in mind), and the numerous ship models.

On warmer days, visit the Botanical Gardens. Start at the Chinese Scholar's Garden with its dramatic black pagoda and pond, then wander the grounds. It's compact, and can be done easily in an hour.

If you like this sight, you might also like the Children's Museum of Manhattan (#55).

MAKE THE MOST OF YOUR TIME

Take the S40 bus for about 2 miles to the Snug Harbor stop. On really nice days, with older kids accustomed to walking, you cover the distance on foot. It's a nice scenic trip along New York Harbor.

EATS FOR KIDS Get a table with a water view at **R.H. Tugs** (1115 Richmond Terr., tel. 718/447–6369). Across the street from Snug Harbor, it has the best views of New York City's working harbor (yes, it includes tugboats plus barges, freighters, and more). The food is fine, but secondary, as your boat-fascinated brood will be engrossed in the real action happening on the water.

SONY WONDER TECHNOLOGY LAB

From the moment you step into the lobby atrium of the Sony Wonder Technology Lab, you feel the excitement of cutting-edge communication technology.

First kids are invited to make a personal profile that follows them throughout the lab. Then—à la Disney circa 1975—the exhibit uses extensive lighting, color, and sound effects, to send them into cyberspace via a "path" of data that includes email, music, downloads, and more.

Creativity meets whiz-bang gadgetry along the way. As they travel through the lab, kids can engage in activities that simultaneously educate and entertain—like mixing music with electronic instruments, making a movie trailer, or designing a video game. Not surprisingly, they can also test Sony's latest PlayStation games.

Of most interest to older kids and adults are the interactive exhibits such as Robot Zone (programming robots), Animation Studio (learning animation techniques), Virtual

KEEP IN MIND

While it's common-place to find free HD movies playing at museums, you seldom find ones aimed specifically at kids, as the screenings here often are. Call the Events RSVP line to reserve tickets for showings (many on Saturday, but days vary) that usually run an hour or less.

EATS FOR KIDS The enormous Sony building lobby serves as a public atrium and is as good a place as any, if not better, to have a snack or picnic lunch before continuing on your way. Within Sony Plaza, **Starbucks** offers sandwiches and pastries. If you can brave the often long lines, visit **Serendipity 3** (225 E. 60th St., tel. 212/838–3531) for dessert, ice-cream treats, and their famous frozen hot chocolate.

550 Madison Ave., Sony Plaza at 56th St.
Subway: 4, 5, 6, N and R to 59th St/Lexington
Ave.; E, M to 5th Ave.; F to 57th St.

 Free

 Tu–Sa 9:30–5:30

212/833–8100; www.
sonywondertechlab.com

All ages

Surgery (just like it sounds), and the two favorites of all ages: Dance Motion Capture (you dance, a Sony animated character mimics your movements) and WSWL Production Studio (be a part of a television newscast).

On Saturdays and select other days a pair of feature films are screened, one for mature audiences and one for very young children (the latter often featuring popular Nickelodeon characters or their friends from *Sesame Street*).

The Tech in the Plaza workshops are some of the most extraordinary programs of their kind around. Children eight and up get to dismantle a piece of electronic equipment to see what's inside and how it works. These are free and registration isn't required; however, space is limited, so get there early. Other workshops include building robots for ages nine and up and crafts for the youngest kids.

If you like this sight, you may also like F.A.O. Schwarz (#48).

MAKE THE MOST OF YOUR TIME

Tickets are required for admission and are often booked far in advance. Try to book when reservations first open (three months before your desired visit), by calling 212/ 833–8100 Tuesday–Friday, 9 AM–2 PM. A minimal number of same-day tickets are available from the walk-up window beginning at 10 Tuesday through Saturday and noon on Sunday.

SOUTH STREET SEAPORT MUSEUM

9

I t's hard to remember that NYC is a port city, what with all the yellow cabs and bike messengers zooming about on land. But heading to the harbor to view historic vessels like the *Peking* (a large sailing cargo ship) and the *Ambrose* (a "floating lighthouse") at the South Street Seaport Museum is a very real reminder for kids. Doing onboard activities lets your crew see how sailors and the maritime industry worked in previous centuries.

In summer, children nine and up love to do one of the Programs Afloat: The two-hour interactive sails on the *Pioneer* schooner have everyone pitching in to man the boat as kids learn about the history of the harbor and environmental responsibility. On a one-hour version, they discover the hidden corners of New York's working waterfront from the deck of the *W.O. Decker* (a 1930 tugboat built in Queens). For older teens and adults, the extended four-hour trip on the tug explores what feels like every crevice of the NY area waterways, including industrial, archaeological, and wildlife sights.

Rotating shows in the museum's exhibit space often have a maritime theme: Past ones have featured memorabilia from the cruise liner *Normandie* and Franklin Delano Roosevelt's

KEEP IN MIND For children under 10, one of the most compelling reasons to visit the area is more about air than water. Little Airplane Productions (207 Front St., tel. 212/965–8999)—the producers of shows including *The Wonder Pets!*—opens its studios to kids on Tuesdays and Thursdays (and occasional Saturdays) for an interactive tour of the creative process. Inside a gorgeously restored brownstone, kids learn step-by-step how a preschool show is created and get to do hands-on activities including drawing, designing, animating, and being the voice-over for an in-process design.

Pier 16 Visitors' Center, 12 Fulton St.
Subway: 2, 3, 4, 5, A, C, J, M, Z to Fulton St.

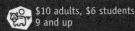 $10 adults, $6 students
9 and up

 Daily 10–6

212/748-8600;
southstreetseaportmuseum.org

3 and up

personal collection of model ships. Yet there are often off-topic surprises, including exhibitions dedicated to folk art or the recent photo installation on the Occupy Wall Street movement. Though interesting, these generally aren't worth the entrance fee alone.

Other programs run by the museum for children include a toddler playgroup, workshops teaching basic sailors' skills (such as navigation or knot tying), crafts programs, and peeks into the environmental world of the East River.

Alas, this area's subway station (Fulton Street) is the only remnant of the East Coast's largest and most important wholesale fish market: Fulton Fish Market, which operated from 1822 to the 1950s. However, the romance of the sea is still very alive here as long as you dodge the generic commercialism.

If you like this sight, you might also like the New York Aquarium (#28).

MAKE THE MOST OF YOUR TIME

Review their website in advance to pick the day and time of your visit. Many of the most enjoyable activities require reservations and book up quickly.

EATS FOR KIDS Go local by walking a block up to Front and Beekman Streets. You'll find several original, non-chain restaurants that cover the four kid food groups—like pizza at **Il Brigante** (214 Front St., 212/285–0222), sandwiches at **Stella Maris** (213 Front St., 212/233–2417), pub food at **Jeremy's Ale House** (228 Front St., 212/964–3537), and chicken fingers at **Cowgirl Seahorse** (259 Front St., 212/608–7873).

Of all the city's zoos, this is the only one that has—for better or worse—retained its Old World feel. On the upside it feels intimate and low key, like a vintage European zoo. You can sit for hours without any crowds; there are no lines; the buildings are low-slung, covered in ivy; and the landscaping makes winding paths. Perhaps the biggest indicator of old-worldliness: the gift shop is so well hidden, and so teeny, you practically have to beg to find it.

The downside? Some of the animals are definitely in enclosures far too small for them. Theoretically, the zoo is working to move them to happier pastures, but for now it can be a bonus for kids who want to feel close enough to touch the whiskers of a big cat.

The Kids' Korral and Children's Center are petting areas with the usual farm animals (picture goats, llamas, and chickens). A quick pony ride is next door as well.

MAKE THE MOST OF YOUR TIME

Plan your day at the zoo so that you don't miss the action during feeding times. Want to check when animals chow down? Feeding schedules are posted at the entry gates.

EATS FOR KIDS The 48 bus stop is a few feet from **Metro Pizza** (1218 Forest Ave., tel. 718/720–3010), where they toss some of healthiest and tastiest pizza on Staten Island. More importantly, it's next door to **The Cookie Jar** (1226 Forest Ave., tel. 718/448–3500), a cubbyhole lined with 200+ cookie jars that would make any collector drool. The cases are filled with 150+ varieties of cookies, bars, and cupcakes, giving your kids something too drool over, too.

614 Broadway, Staten Island
Subway: To Staten Island Ferry terminal, 1 to South
Ferry or 4, 5 to Bowling Green or R to Whitehall

 $8 adults, $5 children 3–14;
free W after 2, parking free

 Daily 10–4:45

718/442–3100; www.
statenislandzoo.org

All ages

Find things that slink and slither at the Carl Kaufeld Serpentarium. Its internationally acclaimed display of reptiles includes one of the most extensive collections of North American rattlesnakes anywhere.

The African Savannah exhibit re-creates the titular ecosystem at twilight and features meerkats, a burrowing python, leopards, bush babies, and rock hyrax—curious creatures that look like rodents but are actually related to elephants. The Tropical Forest exhibit, meanwhile, highlights the endangered South American rainforest and its resident animals. Watch the piranha, spider monkeys, short-tailed leaf-nosed fruit bats, and iguanas in a natural flow of flora and fauna. Over at the Otter Exhibit, see North American river otters perform their antics from above and below the underwater viewing tank.

If you like this sight, you may also like the Queens Zoo (#16).

KEEP IN MIND Clove Lake Park is across the street, and includes a playground, a lake with boat rides, and even an ice-skating rink. Combine this with your zoo trip, ferry ride, and the Cookie Jar snack stop, and you have the perfect Staten Island day.

"Give me your tired, your poor, / Your huddled masses yearning to breathe free. . . ." Many people recognize the opening lines of the 1883 Emma Lazarus poem "The New Colossus," which is inscribed on a plaque inside the Statue of Liberty Museum. And everyone recognizes the sentiment. For more than 100 years this historic monument has served as a universal beacon of hope and opportunity, a symbol of freedom, and a gift of international friendship.

Kids eight and up may enjoy a ranger-led excursion. The Promenade Tour includes the museum in the pedestal's lobby, where the statue's original torch resides, as well as a visit to the promenade, which has great views of the statue and New York Harbor. The Observatory Tour covers much the same ground but adds an elevator ride to the pedestal observatory, with more awesome views, and a lighted view up into the copper interior of the statue. Kids seven to 12 who could be impatient in a lengthy group presentation may be happier taking their own self-guided tour as Junior Rangers; a free booklet, available at the Liberty Island Information Center, walks kids through it.

EATS FOR KIDS Have a big meal before you go, and bring snacks so the kids will be able to hold out until you return to the mainland. Once back, head to Stone Street, a pedestrian-only cobblestone lane lined with great restaurants. There's pizza at **Adrienne's Pizza Bar** (54 Stone St., tel. 212/248–3838), French café pastries and light lunch at **Financier** (62 Stone St., tel. 212/344–5600), pub food at **Stone Street Tavern** (52 Stone St., tel. 212/ 785–5658), and even Swedish cuisine at **Smorgas Chef** (53 Stone St., tel. 212/422–3500).

Liberty Island, New York Harbor
Subway: 4, 5 to Bowling Green, 1 to South
Ferry, R, W to Whitehall

 877/523–9849 ferry tickets and monument
passes, 212/363–3200 NPS information;
www.statuecruises.com, www.nps.gov

 Free; ferry fee including statue
access $17 adult, $9 children
4–12; ferry tickets without
statue access same price

 Daily 9:30–4:50, ferry
daily every 25 min;
closed Dec. 25

4 and up

One of the main reasons to visit the statue, of course, is to inspect this monument to freedom up close. A museum features exhibits detailing how the statue was built, and the promenade, colonnade, and top level of the pedestal offer spectacular views of New York Harbor. Life-size castings of the face and foot of the statue are available for sight-impaired visitors to feel. A timed-pass reservation system is run by the National Park Service for visitors who want to enter the monument. A limited number of timed passes is available from the ferry company daily on a first-come, first-served basis; alternately, get you can get one online at www. statuecruises.com. Timed passes are not required to visit the grounds. As she always has, Lady Liberty welcomes all.

If you like this sight, you may also like Ellis Island (#50).

KEEP IN MIND
Most children under 12 will not have the stamina to do a combo tour of both Liberty and Ellis Island.

MAKE THE MOST OF YOUR TIME Getting tickets far in advance is easy, fast, and a must. Visit www.statuecruises.com to see available dates and times, and to add options like the audio tour or a visit to Ellis Island.

SYMPHONY SPACE

Take a good long look at New York City parents. For every pinstripe-suited mom or clean-cut dad there's at least one tattooed former rocker pushing a stroller. These are parents who cut their teenage teeth at spots like CBGBs, the Beacon, or the Fillmore. Now that their iPods have slightly more Baby Einstein and slightly less Johnny Rotten, they need a venue to indoctrinate their future Rolling Stone. And that's where Symphony Space comes in.

Symphony Space is an incredible misnomer, as this is the site of several rockin' shows. For families, it's anything but a staid classical music spot—although it does have plenty of that for adults. At its heart, it's an Upper West Side institution where kids can dance in the aisles, sing, cheer, get up on stage, and generally prepare for the mosh pit.

During the school year there is at least one family event per week. Kid-friendly bands kick out the jams and get their little fans up and moving. Expect a good mix of evergreen

MAKE THE MOST OF YOUR TIME

On warm days pair your show with some time at Riverside Park, only one block away. Less crowded than Central Park, it's a low-key way to take time out. There are several great playgrounds, meandering paths, and, of course, waterfront views.

EATS FOR KIDS On this patch of Broadway it's hard to find a restaurant that isn't family-friendly. The 24-hour **City Diner** (2441 Broadway, tel. 212/877–2720) is popular for pancakes and diner food 'round the clock. A bit of a walk, but worth it, is **Popover Café** (551 Amsterdam Ave., tel. 212/595–8555). A big basket of fresh popovers and a plate of lemon pancakes will quash any hunger-induced meltdowns.

2537 Broadway between 95th and 96th Sts.
Subway: 1, 2, 3 to 96th St.

 212/864–5400; www.
symphonyspace.org

 Varies by show

 Mostly weekends, varies by show

 2 and up

favorites like Laurie Berkner and Dan Zanes and lesser-known newcomers like Captain Bogg or Salty and The Milkshakes.

Check their schedule for upcoming festivals. Occasionally they will hold free-form events for the whole family, such as the recent Korean Traditional Performing Arts Association Annual Family Program.

During the summer, when most families head out of town or do outdoor activities, the schedule slims down and focuses less on live performances. It's mostly a place that comes alive during the school year.

If you like this sight, you may also like the New Victory Theater (#29).

KEEP IN MIND The other wildly popular event that takes place here is the New York International Children's Film Festival. Tickets for showings of these engaging and creative animated films sell out almost the minute they go on sale, with some seats available same-day. If you're going to be in town sometime between December and February, this is definitely worth attending. Get on their email list for first notification.

UNION SQUARE PARK

nion Square was named for its location at the "union"—or less poetically, the intersection—of Fourth Avenue and Broadway. But another meaning of the word crept in during the late 19th and early 20th centuries when labor unions protested in the area.

If that was more of a teachable moment than you or your kids bargained for, don't worry. The historical aspects of Union Square Park only assert themselves in subtle ways— sidewalk plaques on the southeast and southwest sides of the park recall its history from the 1600s to 1800s, and there are a few statues and a beautiful fountain. But beyond that the definition of "union" most resonant here is that New Yorkers and visitors simply love getting together and walking, shopping, reading, or people-watching in and around the 6½-acre park.

Strolling the perimeter—an entirely flat mile-long stretch—is a good way to absorb the ambience. Walk north on the Union Square West side of the park to take in the popular Greenmarket that continues around the north end bound by 17th Street. Although you

KEEP IN MIND Two more literary spots in the neighborhood worth your kids' time are **Books of Wonder** (18 W. 18th St. and Broadway, tel. 212/989–3270), a charming indie shop for children where you might spot authors who haven't yet made it to the big chains; and **Forbidden Planet** (840 Broadway, tel. 212/473–1576) which has the most impressive selection of comic books and comic memorabilia in New York, perhaps even in the galaxy.

Bound by Union Square East and West, W. 14th and W. 17th Sts.
Subway: 4, 5, 6, N, Q, R, W to Union Sq./14th St.

 Free

 212/788-7900 Greenmarket information; www.grownyc.org

Union Square Greenmarket
M, W, F, Sa 8-6

 3 and up

likely won't be lugging groceries home, there's no harm in grazing the breads and cheese and produce while you're here.

You'll notice as you walk that the Union Square West and East sides of the park are flanked by all manner of chains-restaurants, clothing shops, office-, and baby-supply stores—which are quite useful and really do nothing to detract from the area. In fact, one of the better Barnes & Noble stores in the entire national chain sits on the north end of the park.

A good place to finish up your walk is on the south side at 14th Street, where the concrete steps serve as perhaps the best spot in the neighborhood to picnic. If you didn't pick up any fixings at the Greenmarket, a Whole Foods conveniently looms across the street.

If you like this sight, you may also like the Carl Schurz Park (#60).

EATS FOR KIDS

Before Whole Foods came to the south side of Union Square park, **Garden of Eden Gourmet** (7 East 16th St., tel. 212/ 255-4200) was already there dispensing healthy grab-and-go foods. Very child-friendly and with a humorous country diner feel, **Chat 'n Chew** (10 East 16th St., tel. 243-1616) has good mac-and-cheese and fish tacos.

MAKE THE MOST OF YOUR TIME Delightful for kids
and grown-ups because it is almost literally a maze of books, **The Strand** (826 Broadway, tel. 212/473-1452), a five-minute walk south of Union Square Park, is not to be missed. Claiming to have 18 miles of new, used, rare, and out-of-print books, this is by far NYC's biggest indie bookstore.

4

Kids may not "get" abstract concepts like nationalism and political boundaries, or lofty goals like international human rights. But they get sending postcards to friends and family with stamps you can't buy anywhere else in the world. They get seeing people in enchanting national dress, like flowing gold saris from India and brightly colored dashikis from South Africa. And they definitely get listening to words being translated into tens of other languages instantly.

As you approach the headquarters, point out the 192 different flags representing 192 different nations arranged alphabetically (from Afghanistan to Zimbabwe). Then, explain to your kids how it may feel like they are still in New York, but they are actually entering a different country—international land belonging to those 191 nations complete with its own security forces and post office with its own postage. You might want to play "I Spy" at the massive stained-glass window in the lobby, a Chagall creation. Kids will find

KEEP IN MIND

Before you leave, step into the post office to send home a souvenir: a postcard with stamps issued exclusively by the United Nations. Kids can also make personalized stamps featuring their own photo.

MAKE THE MOST OF YOUR TIME
While it's easy enough to walk here from the subway, you might want to consider a bus ride, too, as the U.N. is right next to the East River. The M15 and M50 buses will drop you off and pick you up in front of the building.

1st Ave. and 46th St.
Subway: 4, 5, 6, 7 to Grand Central Station

 $16 adults, $11 students,
$9 children 5–12

212/963–8687; www.un.org/tours

 Guided and audio tours M–F
9:45–4:45; audio tour Sa–Su
10–4:15 except Jan–Feb

8 and up, tour 5 and up

symbols of peace and music in the design. And be sure to show them Foucault's pendulum and teach them that it proves the earth rotates.

Families with children five and up should begin by taking the tour. In a relatively quick 45 minutes you'll see the General Assembly, where the member nations meet, and (subject to the construction schedule) the Security Council Chamber, Trustee Council Chamber, Economic and Social Council Chamber, Rose Garden, and public concourse. There may also be a stop to see the many gifts member nations have donated over the years.

If you like this sight, you may also like Ellis Island (#50).

EATS FOR KIDS Skip the UN Delegates dining room. It may have views of the East River, but it also has a strict dress code (no jeans or shorts, jackets for men). So it's not exactly a spot to spread out coloring books. Instead, head back toward First Avenue, where you'll find affordable restaurants for all tastes. For a treat, walk a few blocks to **Buttercup Bakeshop** (973 2nd Ave., tel. 212/350–4144) to sample the city's best Rice Crispy treats and 20+ varieties of cupcakes.

VICTORIAN GARDENS

3

In summer, Wollman Rink transforms into an amusement park with quaint but enjoyable rides, greasy food, and some boardwalk-style games where you may (or may not) impress your progeny by winning a dinky prize. In other words, it resembles just about any county fair you've ever visited

A few rides are standouts. On the Fun Slide, kids zip down a plastic slide atop a cloth sack (attendants will help position younger ones at the top if you're not riding with them). Encourage your child to do this one a few times in succession if there isn't a long line, as eventually there will be. Mini Mouse is a roller coaster with no thrills whatsoever, but its quick turns will delight the little ones, especially if you scream and act terrified. The whimsically named Family Swinger is the most county-fairish ride, with 16 child seats and 16 adult ones that are lofted through the air at dazzling heights. Kids are permitted to take off their sandals or flip-flops before boarding this one, as inevitably footwear goes sailing.

KEEP IN MIND A wristband for unlimited rides is generally a better deal for children. However, if your kids are over six or seven and prone to doing rides alone, you'll get better value by taking the admission-only option for yourself.

Wollman Rink, Central Park
Subway: 1, A, B, C, D to 59th St./
Columbus Circle; F to 57th St./6th Ave.

212/982-2229; www.
victoriangardensnyc.com

$20.50 weekdays admission
with unlimited rides for guests
over 36" tall, $23.50 weekends;
$6.50 weekdays admission only,
$7.50 weekends

June–Sept, M–F 11–7, Sa 10–9,
Su 10–8; Oct–May hrs vary,
check website for details

3 and up

Children under 42" must ride with an adult on a few of the park's dozen rides, including Aeromax ("airplanes" offering views of the park), Kite Flyer (free flight in a reclining position, and perhaps the most fun mother–daughter or father–son ride in the place), and Rockin' Tug (a whirling and turning boat ride adults may want to skip).

On weekends there are at least four shows a day by well-practiced children's entertainers. Two favorites that return year after year are *Jenny's Big Hula Hoop Show* (remarkable feats with 20+ hula hoops at once) and *King Henry's Magic Show*. Recently the entertainment options have broadened to include clowns, Wild West tricks, card tricks, and the like.

If you like this sight, you may also like Coney Island (#52).

MAKE THE MOST OF YOUR TIME

Get here as early as you can and plan on staying about three hours. After that, almost everything has been done twice. Get a hand stamp for all-day reentry.

EATS FOR KIDS Outside food isn't allowed inside, but there are several wholesome and delicious places around Central Park South. Stop at one before or after a trip here, and you'll save your kids from overpriced hot dogs and pizza. **Whole Foods** (10 Columbus Circle, tel. 212/823–9600) has a popular eat-in area with fresh-made all-natural pizzas, ethnic food bars (Indian, Chinese, Mexican), and rotisserie meats with vegetable sides.

WAVE HILL

The American Museum of Natural History (#68), the National Park System, and teddy bears all owe a giant debt of gratitude to Wave Hill.

Back in the day (read: before income taxes) NYC's upscale residents escaped the heat by going to their summer compounds on the Hudson River. Wave Hill, a few minutes from Manhattan, is not only one of the most impressive of these, it's also rumored to be the place where young Teddy Roosevelt developed his passion for nature and nurtured the roots of his future conservation efforts (his family rented the home from 1870 to 1871). Overlooking the Hudson River and Palisades, this public garden spans 23 acres and includes a greenhouse, rock garden, lawns, an aquatic garden, Wave Hill House, education center, café, shop, and plenty of benches, picnic spots, pergolas, lawn chairs, and other lounging features.

Today, families visiting on weekends will find it's one of the easiest ways for parents to have a truly tranquil moment while the kids are kept happily engaged. Every Saturday

MAKE THE MOST OF YOUR TIME

Before you settle your plans, pick out a day with a good weather forecast, and keep in mind that Wave Hill is closed most Mondays.

EATS FOR KIDS Eating beforehand or bringing a picnic is the best food option for children. There is a walled outdoor **picnic area.** The **small café** is the only on-site food outlet, and while its local organic ingredients are delectable, it's best for adults (unless your kids fantasize about cured Thai salmon on seven-grain bread with lemongrass crème fraîche).

24 W. 249th St. and Independence Ave., Bronx
Subway: 1 to 242nd St.; A to 207th St.

718/549003200; www.wavehill.org

$8 adults, $4 students, $2 children 6 and up; free select T and Sa mornings, $8 on-site parking, free shuttle

Mar 15–Oct 31, 9–5:30 T–Su; Nov 1–Mar 14, 9–4:30 T–Su

 All ages

and Sunday Wave Hill holds an art workshop open to children of all ages. These begin with an outdoor activity (in warmer months), giving children a chance to observe the natural world with the help of the artist leader. They then go indoors to a large craft room where they'll leisurely make that day's project.

Even without the workshops, there's plenty to entice both parents and families. To school-age children, Wave Hill is a secret garden where they can look for fairies and butterflies; a castle where they can pretend to be royalty; a fortress where they can protect their loyal subjects; or an enchanted forest where they can play hide-and-seek.

If you like this sight, you may also like the New York Botanical Garden (#27).

KEEP IN MIND Getting here without a car is simple. Wave Hill provides free shuttles to pick people up at the 242nd Street subway stop (on the 1 line) and Metro North (Riverdale station). Generally these run hourly, but check their website for the latest details, as they can change seasonally. It is an easy five-minute walk from the Henry Hudson Parkway/252nd Street bus stop, where numerous express buses drop off passengers. Bx7, Bx10, BxM1, and BxM2 all stop there.

YANKEE STADIUM

The House that Ruth Built is now in pieces all over the world. After the stadium was torn down, bits of the "rubble," such as the blue seats, were sold off to collectors. The new, completely modern arena bears little resemblance to the old, with upscale restaurants, snack delivery to any seat in the place (for a room service–like surcharge, of course) and luxury suites. But the spirit of fans rooting for the home team managed to make the move intact.

The best way to experience the stadium is, not surprisingly, to go to a game. The park opens two hours before each one, and kids can often score an autograph from a player before the end of batting practice if they get close to the field. Before the game, walk around Monument Park, which contains plaques and memorials to the all-time greats: Mickey Mantle, Joe DiMaggio, Lou Gehrig, and the Babe, as well as a tribute plaque remembering September 11.

MAKE THE MOST OF YOUR TIME

The subway isn't just the cheapest way to get here, it's the primo way. Riding the train up to the stadium (particularly the 4 train) and being among fans festooned in every conceivable stripe and color of Yankee-wear will get you pumped for the game ahead.

EATS FOR KIDS One distinct improvement in the new Yankee Stadium is the food. Forget having only old hot dogs and stale Cracker Jacks. Now there are several sit-down offerings, including **Hard Rock Cafe** and **NYY Steak.** There's an entire range of quick-serve foods from popular local and national brands, including **Melissa's** for fresh fruit and salads, **Brother Jimmy's BBQ, Popcorn Indiana,** and for parents, **Beers of the World.**

1 E. 161st St., Bronx
Subway: 4, B, D to 161st St./Yankee Stadium

Games $14 and up; tours
$20 adult, $15 children
14 and under

Tours M–Sa 9–4:40 except
when team plays at home

718/293-4300; www.
newyorkyankees.com

5 and up

Tickets are easier to come by now that there's more room in the stadium. Still, planning in advance is always a good idea, especially for popular games. And unless you are ready to pay top dollar, forget Subway Series seats (aka when the Yankees and the Mets face off).

Take the tour if you can't make the game. The Classic Tour lasts an hour and goes to three places: New York Yankees Museum, Monument Park, and the Yankees dugout.

You can also opt for tickets to the city's two minor-league teams, the Brooklyn Cyclones and Staten Island Yankees. These often delight kids more than the major leagues, with the action so close and fun events just for kids (*see* Coney Island #52).

If you like this sight, you may also like Basketball for Kids (#67).

KEEP IN MIND The crowds in the stadium interior can be intense, so guest services provides wristbands to help children identify their seat locations. Look for the Tag-A-Kid guest services booths throughout the stadium to get a wristband. Also, check the Yankees website to take note of games where promotions or giveaways are scheduled. Caps, stuffed toys, and trading cards are among the items handed out, sometimes only to kids 12 and under (which will make them feel particularly special).

CLASSIC GAMES

"I SEE SOMETHING YOU DON'T SEE, AND IT IS BLUE." Stuck for a way to get your youngsters to settle down in a museum? Sit them on a bench in the middle of a room and play this vintage favorite. The leader gives just one clue—the color—and everybody guesses away.

"I'M GOING TO THE GROCERY STORE . . ." The first player begins, "I'm going to the grocery store and I'm going to buy . . .," finishing the sentence with the name of an object, found in grocery stores, that begins with the letter "A." The second player repeats what the first player has said, and adds the name of another item that starts with "B." The third player repeats everything that has been said so far and adds something that begins with "C," and so on through the alphabet. Anyone who skips or misremembers an item is out (or decide up front that you'll give hints to all who need 'em). You can modify the theme depending on where you're going that day, as "I'm going to X and I'm going to see . . ."

FAMILY ARK Noah had his ark—here's your chance to build your own. It's easy: Just start naming animals and work your way through the alphabet, from antelope to zebra.

PLAY WHILE YOU WAIT

NOT THE GOOFY GAME Have one child name a category. (Some ideas: first names, last names, animals, countries, friends, feelings, foods, hot or cold items, clothing.) Then take turns naming things that fall into it. You're out if you name something that doesn't belong in the category or if you can't think of another item to add. When only one person remains, start again. Choose categories depending on where you're going or where you've been: historic topics if you've seen a historic sight, animal topics before or after the zoo, upside-down things if you've been to the circus, and so on. Make the game harder by choosing category items in A-B-C order.

DRUTHERS How do your kids really feel about things? Just ask. "Would you rather eat worms or hamburgers? Hamburgers or candy?" Choose serious and silly topics-and have fun!

BUILD A STORY "Once upon a time there lived . . ." Finish the sentence and ask the rest of your family, one at a time, to add another sentence or two. If you can, record the narrative so you can enjoy your creation again and again.

GOOD TIMES GALORE

WIGGLE & GIGGLE Give your kids a chance to stick out their tongues at you. Start by making a face, then have the next person imitate you and add a gesture of his own-snapping fingers, winking, clapping, sneezing, or the like. The next person mimics the first two and adds a third gesture, and so on.

JUNIOR OPERA During a designated period of time, have your kids sing everything they want to say.

THE QUIET GAME Need a good giggle or a moment of calm to figure out your route? The driver sets a time limit and everybody must be silent. The last person to make a sound wins.

MANY THANKS

Thanks to my parents Barbara and Larry for making me almost as funny as they are.

Another thanks to my dad, who made sure at an early age that I understood a writer's torment and who never once suggested that it should scare me.

Maria Hart, I have known good editors and good people, and you are both.

To Toby, my wife of two decades, thanks again for helping me type my college thesis the night before it was due, and for every moment since when you've rescued me.

To Libby, Maya, and Felix, thanks for letting me be your dad. I can think of no other kids I would rather go around the city with.

—Paul Eisenberg